THE MIDDLEBURY COLLEGE MUSEUM OF ART AND ITS FRIENDS

The Middlebury College Museum of Art and Its Friends

EMMIE DONADIO

Middlebury College Museum of Art, Vermont

This catalogue was published in conjunction with the exhibition *Friends Bearing Gifts: 40 Years of Acquisitions from the Friends of the Art Museum*, on view at the Middlebury College Museum of Art, September 17 – December 12, 2010.

Published by the Middlebury College Museum of Art
Middlebury, Vermont

ISBN 978–1–928825–08–1

FRONT COVER: Govaert Flinck, *Portrait of a Man* (detail), 17th century, oil on panel, 21⅝ × 16¼ inches. Gift of the Friends of Art, 1981.006 (Photo: Arthur Evans)

BACK COVER: Giuseppe De Nittis, *Study for Alle Corse*, c. 1874, oil on panel, 5 × 9¼ inches. Purchase with funds provided by the Friends of Art Acquisition Fund and the Christian A. Johnson Memorial Fund, 1989.007 (Photo: Tad Merrick)

FRONTISPIECE: *Caparisoned Horse*, Chinese, Eastern Wei dynasty (534–550), polychrome ceramic, 12¾ × 12½ × 7¾ inches. Purchase with funds provided by the Friends of Art Acquisition Fund, 2004.015 (Photo: Ken Burris)

Contents

Statuette of Venus, Roman, Hadrianic Period, c. 118–136 C.E., bronze with traces of gilding, h. 5½ inches. Purchase with funds provided by the Friends of Art Acquisition Fund, 2005.053. (Photo: Tad Merrick)

Preface

On this auspicious occasion, it is a great privilege to acknowledge my indebtedness to the work of my predecessors. When I came to Middlebury in 1985 I knew that the College had an extraordinary record of achievement in its academic sphere. But what has impressed me over the years, and continues to impress me today, is the extreme dedication of its local friends and its loyal alumni. They have made our goals into realities, our mission into a shared accomplishment.

As Emmie Donadio makes clear in the essay that follows, any survey of the Friends of the Art Museum is tantamount to a history of the Christian A. Johnson Memorial Gallery and of its successor, which now houses that Gallery, the Middlebury College Museum of Art. Our Friends have been essential to all of our transitions and all of our efforts. From the inception of the mission to create a permanent art collection for the College to the present day—when we can be justifiably proud of our Museum, accredited by the American Association of Museums—we have had the benefit of the ongoing generosity, care and attention of a remarkably stable group of Middlebury families. They know who they are, and as you read this publication, you too will be reminded or come to know who they are. A relatively small group of benefactors has aided us immeasurably in our enterprise in these past decades.

But they have not acted alone.

I believe it is fair to say that these benefactors have been impressed from the start by the community—the small village, as it were—that has rallied around the inauguration of the Gallery and continues to maintain its vitality as a local resource. To you, the members of the local community of the Friends of Art—those named and unnamed in the following pages—we are also immensely grateful. The record presented here should stand as a testament to what can be accomplished through relatively modest, but consistent donations. And without your faithful presence throughout the period of our existence, our public would not have been as distinctive and recognizable as it surely is. I know that I can speak for my predecessors A. Richard Turner and David Bumbeck in telling you how much we have enjoyed the hours of convivial and productive fellowship that we have shared.

The Friends of the Art Museum, the College's first town and gown association, has been truly successful in realizing its mission to bring visual art to the attention and awareness of the community at large. We look forward to bringing this remarkable history of accomplishment into the future as we now celebrate our forty-year anniversary.

Richard H. Saunders
Director and Walter Cerf Distinguished College Professor
Middlebury College of Museum of Art

Acknowledgments

This publication and the exhibition which it is meant to accompany represent in themselves an Acknowledgment writ large. With forty years of history behind us, we now pay tribute to our unfailingly loyal and supportive community of Friends of Art: alumni of Middlebury College and citizens of its town who have committed themselves to serving this important cultural institution ever since its inception. Like any organization that depends upon the generosity and hard work of those who believe in its mission, the Middlebury College Museum of Art is honored to have this opportunity to thank its supporters.

To the Christian A. Johnson Endeavor Foundation and to Julie Johnson Kidd '67 and her mother, Charlotte, we owe our very existence. The Christian A. Johnson Memorial Gallery, formerly located across campus in the Christian A. Johnson Memorial Building, was our first incarnation. The Christian A. Johnson Endeavor Foundation continues to provide generous and substantial support for both the Museum acquisitions and exhibitions programs. The visual arts at the College—in both their curricular and public sphere—have been inestimably and indelibly enhanced by the philanthropy of the Johnson family.

The ambitious and far-seeing administration of Middlebury President James I. Armstrong, his highly able and accomplished Vice President Walter E. Brooker, and their colleague, first Gallery Director A. Richard Turner, demonstrated the wisdom and skill needed to set us on a secure and productive course, and we owe them our deepest respect and gratitude. Their successors—Gallery Directors David Bumbeck and Richard H. Saunders; Presidents Olin Robison, Timothy Light, John M. McCardell, Jr., and Ronald D. Liebowitz—have maintained and overseen the growth and flourishing of what for the past eighteen years has been the Middlebury College Museum of Art. Our home in the Kevin P. Mahaney '85 Center for the Arts has permitted us to show the results of this steady vision in a long series of extraordinarily handsome installations and exhibitions. The outdoor sculpture collection that appears in many sites across the campus may also be considered a result of their strategic planning.

The generous benefactors on whom we have regularly relied are named and given thanks in the pages that follow. Among those whose long association with the Friends goes back to the group's founding are Julie Johnson Kidd '67, Robert C. Graham, Jr. '64, Robert P. Youngman '64 and Barbara P. Youngman, Frederick W. Lapham III '70 and Martha Lapham, and the George Seybolt Family.

On this fortieth anniversary, we also call attention to the efforts of some past and present leaders of the Friends of the Art Museum whose capacity for sustained engagement has been extraordinary. Betty Fishman, Rick Lapham, Bob Kingsley, Peggy Keith, and Dinny Faurote—to name but five—have together provided nearly four times forty years in service to the Friends. Many others whose names may not appear in the text that follows (or in the Appendix, where Chairs of the group are named) have contributed to our record of accomplishment. And to them—and you—we also owe a debt of gratitude: the annual dues-paying Friends of Art and Friends of the Art Museum who have succeeded in summoning, year in and year out, the energy and enthusiasm that enable us to pursue our public mission.

The author would also like to take this occasion to recognize the essential and invaluable assistance of the following individuals who aided in bringing this publication to fruition: first and foremost, Margaret Wallace, museum registrar and publications manager, who ably and generously oversaw the enterprise through all of its many incarnations; Christopher Ross, text editor, and Christopher Kuntze, designer; Robert Reiff Intern Isabel Rey McWilliams '10 and Museum Intern Alexandra Guynn '12, whose cheerfulness and exuberance helped keep the project bright through the dark seasons; and Summer Intern Esme Lutz '12.5, whose diligence, alertness, and enthusiasm could be counted on throughout the hot and humid final push.

For generously answering many inquiries, on the telephone and in person, I want to thank the following: A. Richard Turner, Betty Fishman, David Bumbeck, Helen Reiff, Bob Kingsley, Glenn Andres, John Hunisak, Rick and Martha Lapham, Richard Saunders, Tim Etchells, Susan Kavanagh, Megan Foley Williamson, and Janie Chester Young.

It would be difficult to imagine how Danielle Rougeau, assistant curator of Special Collections in Middlebury's Davis Family Library, could have been more helpful or accommodating in making available the essential primary sources and documents on which this history is based. Her expert assistance has been immensely valuable to all of us who have had the pleasure of working with her.

To the alumni, faculty colleagues, and other authors of the label texts accompanying the works of art on view in the exhibition *Friends Bearing Gifts*, we offer our gratitude for the richness and diversity of their voices and viewpoints.

Finally, to all who have become members of the Friends of Art and the Art Museum in the forty years of its existence—those who have served on its committees, voted for its gifts to the collection, traveled on its trips, participated in its events, and paid their dues—this publication is forever dedicated.

Emmie Donadio
Chief Curator

Fig. 1. Vice President Walter E. Brooker '37 addresses the crowd at the inauguration of the Christian A. Johnson Memorial Building, 1968. College Archives, Special Collections Middlebury College

The Middlebury College Museum of Art and its Friends

The history we celebrate here begins, most precisely, with the opening of the Christian A. Johnson Memorial Building. Completed in the spring of 1968, it housed the Department of Fine Arts and the College's Department of Music. A gift of the Christian A. Johnson Endeavor Foundation, the building was "generously donated to the College for the furtherance of creative and scholarly activities in Music and Art in memory of an admirable gentleman by his family."[1] Among that Johnson family was recent alumna Julie Johnson '67, who, along with her mother, Charlotte, wanted to leave a lasting legacy to the College.[2] (Figs. 1–4)

Conceived in an architectural style aptly designated "brutalist," the bilaterally symmetrical design of Jean Paul Carlhian (of the Boston firm Shepley Bulfinch Richardson and Abbott), the Johnson building contained the Christian A. Johnson Memorial Gallery, art studios, and classrooms. These were complemented by a two-story concert hall (the twin of the gallery) and music rehearsal studios. The first art exhibition in the facility, mounted in spring 1968, was a retrospective of works by Arthur K. D. Healy, the driving force who had chaired the Fine Arts Department and who was stepping down after a twenty-five-year teaching career at Middlebury. (Fig. 5)

At the celebratory inaugural festivities for the building, in fall 1969, Thomas P. F. Hoving, Jr., director of New York's Metropolitan Museum of Art, used the occasion—in the paradigmatic manner of the waning years of the Vietnam War—to excoriate the current

Fig. 2. Portrait of Christian A. Johnson by Mara McAfee, oil on canvas, 16 ×15 inches. Courtesy of the Christian A. Johnson Endeavor Foundation

Fig. 3. Portrait of Mrs. Christian (Charlotte) A. Johnson by James Pollard, oil on canvas, 16 × 15 inches. Courtesy of the Christian A. Johnson Endeavor Foundation

Fig. 4. Julie Johnson '67 at the inaugural ceremony, 1968. College Archives, Special Collections Middlebury College

Fig. 6. Thomas P. F. Hoving speaks at the inauguration of Christian A. Johnson Memorial Building, 1968. College Archives, Special Collections Middlebury College

Fig. 5. Installation view of Arthur K. D. Healy Retrospective exhibition, Spring 1968. College Archives, Special Collections Middlebury College

national administration, stating that we the people would be better off governed by artists and poets than by the current crop of politicians:

Not too many years ago, I would have spoken about the building's essence and the forthcoming contributions in terms of a sort of ivory-towered preserve, isolated, insulated, protected and removed [from] other streams of life. . . . Today that is not possible. You could not make the wonderful place ivory-towered, removed and protected if you wanted to. . . . Those young people who emerge from this place will be the only ones best-trained and qualified to go into all levels of government and all parts of the democratic life. . . . A congress and a cabinet filled with art historians, artists, musicians and musicologists would have done far better, I think, than the deep-thinking clutch of politicians, lawyers, and businessmen that have made such a distinguished record for the past 5 years.[3] (Fig. 6)

Hoving's call for artists and art educators to immerse themselves in "the democratic life" was soon heeded. In addition to the steady stream of Middlebury alumni who would pass through the Johnson Building and go on to prominence in the public sphere of arts and letters, it was not long before the Friends of Art were summoned into existence. For more than forty years the contributions of this group of civic leaders, alumni, and extended Middlebury family have enriched the cultural life of the Middlebury community and, through their ongoing activities, served as a model of town-gown relations. President of the College James I. Armstrong had made it a priority of his administration to strengthen the College's academic departments, particularly in the areas

Fig. 7. President James I. Armstrong at the inauguration of the Johnson Building, 1968. College Archives, Special Collections Middlebury College

Fig. 8. Dr. A. Richard Turner, 1975 (Photo: Erik Borg)

of languages, classics, and art. To that end he had tapped the faculty at Princeton, bringing among other distinguished appointees Professor A. Richard Turner "to enhance the Fine Arts program."[4] (Figs. 7–8) A scholar of Leonardo da Vinci and the Florentine Renaissance, Turner was also a dynamic proponent of the art of the present. As chair of the Department of Fine Arts he was, in effect, the executive officer of the Johnson Gallery. He oversaw the acquisitions, worked to bring exhibitions to the campus, and identified and pursued donors for the new facility and its nascent art collection. Besides working to attract loans and funding from alumni and the local community, Turner made similar demands upon himself, since he came from a family that set a high standard for gift giving. Indeed, what is among the Middlebury collection's finest paintings is a 1969 gift from the director's mother: Theodore Rousseau's *The Gorge at Apremonte.* The Barbizon School canvas was given to the collection by Mrs. Louis A. Turner in memory of her father, Frank Jewett Mather, Jr. Mather, for whom the College Art Association named its annual award for art journalism, had been a widely read critic in the early twentieth century, writing for *The New York Evening Post, Burlington Magazine,* and *The Atlantic Monthly,* among numerous other publications. He was among the members of the first generation of art historians

teaching at Princeton and had also served as director of the Princeton University Art Museum from 1922 to 1946.[5]

Soon after he assumed his responsibilities as chair of the Middlebury Fine Arts Department, Turner laid the groundwork for the town-gown committee, whose purpose, as outlined in a letter to Mrs. Christian A. Johnson, was to provide the community with a "continuing program of loan exhibitions; openings to all loan exhibitions for members only; and lectures and special events at the Johnson Building." In addition, the Friends would "extend a warm welcome to school groups at the Johnson Gallery" and "circulat[e] exhibitions for area schools." Lastly, through their support for new acquisitions, the members of the organization would be able to "bring delight to generations of Middlebury students and our neighbors."[6]

Mrs. Johnson was to become honorary chair of the Friends of Art. Her daughter Julie would also become one of the College's most generous and active supporters in the foundation of the permanent art collection and art programming at the College.

Fig. 9. David Bumbeck demonstrates printing techniques to local youth, 1969. College Archives, Special Collections Middlebury College

True to their stated purpose, in their first year the Friends of Art sponsored—along with the Middlebury Union High School humanities department—a traveling exhibition of original art works that circulated to area high schools. They also organized Saturday morning art classes for some forty elementary school children in the community. These artmaking sessions were conducted by students and faculty at the College.[7] (Fig. 9) The Johnson Building itself became a stimulus for community-wide cultural enrichment. There was perceptible excitement in town for the new promise of urbanity, international culture, and opportunities for ongoing education that this College facility offered to every member of the family. Here was a nexus between the local community and the world beyond the rural setting, and anyone who had been anywhere or had a modicum of cultural sophistication responded to the invitation to be numbered among the Friends of Art.

From its origin, the Friends flourished under Turner's inspired and energetic leadership. Their efforts were strongly supported by President Armstrong, his wife, Carol, who served on the first board of directors of the group, and their daughter Carol (Cary) A. Tall, who kept the minutes, compiled the first *Annual Reports*, assisted in the management of loans, and curated several outstanding exhibitions. Also essential to the success of the Friends from the outset were the College's vice president and chief development officer Walter E. Brooker '37 and his wife, Barbara-Ann Carrick Brooker '40. As both Turner and his successor David Bumbeck recall, the Brookers were indispensable and indefatigable in the energies they devoted to the successful launch of the College's new endeavor.

With the administration's strong support and its belief in the importance of building an art collection for Middlebury, the Friends group was able to devote all of its membership funds to acquisitions. Entertainment expenses incurred by the activities of the group from its earliest days were absorbed by the Friends themselves. Maintenance of the group's records and assistance with publications, mailings, and programs were shared by the College's development office and the faculty and staff of the Fine Arts Department.

The first chair of the group, Mrs. Samuel W. (Betty) Fishman, of Vergennes, described

Fig. 10. Betty Fishman, President Armstrong, and Alice Dibble, 1970. College Archives, Special Collections Middlebury College

Fig. 11. Emcee Harold Curtiss at the annual Purchase Party, 1993 (Photo: Benjamin Garver '89)

by Turner as one of those "larger than life personalities,"[8] conducted the first meeting of the Friends in January 1969. Letters from President Armstrong and from Turner, congratulating her on her splendid and spirited leadership, are included in the College archives. (Fig. 10) With Betty as chair, Mrs. Christian A. Johnson as honorary chair, and Turner himself at the helm of the gallery, there was an abundance of productive cooperation. In addition, the first board comprised of local residents counted in its ranks artists, art historians, art and antique dealers, educators, lawyers, and physicians. Their energy, talent, and flair succeeded in getting the Friends off to a highly auspicious beginning.

Besides Mrs. Armstrong, Mr. Harold M. Curtiss—art collector, bon vivant, and former principal of the Sidwell Friends School in our nation's capital—served on the first executive committee. (Fig. 11) "Curt," who for decades owned the Waybury Inn in East Middlebury and ran Camp Keewaydin on the shores of nearby Lake Dunmore, was chair of the Friends for many years. He became the unforgettable (and often mischievous) emcee

at many Friends functions for the next three decades. With Robert Kingsley, who co-managed the Waybury Inn with Curtiss (and was a former government official on his way to becoming an attorney when he decamped D.C. for Vermont), the leadership had not only "bigger than life" personalities, but also seasoned managers who could be counted on to maintain the momentum.

Others on the board included Mrs. Alice Dibble, a remarkably lively art and antiques dealer. (Fig. 12) According to Turner, whose memory of her is as sharp as the woman's wit was reported to be, Dibble once addressed her monthly check to the local Shoreham phone company "to the Worst Goddamn Phone Company in the Nation." It was duly cashed.[9] Others recall Dibble, summoned into action to install exhibitions in the gallery—a favor Turner was often in those days compelled to ask—hammering hardware into the walls while wearing her customary white gloves, and swearing all the while like a sailor.[10] Dibble's art establishment continues to this day as Lapham and Dibble, under the leadership of Frederick W. Lapham III '70 and his wife, Martha, who were close friends of Dibble. (Fig. 13) Also on the first executive committee were Mr. Francis Kelley, future principal of Middlebury Union High School, and Mr. Arthur Williams, director of the Vermont Council on the Arts.

Fig. 12. Alice Dibble, December 4, 1977 (Photo: Erik Borg)

Fig. 13. Connie Bumbeck, Martha Lapham, David Bumbeck, and Rick Lapham, 1980. (Photo: Erik Borg)

Fig. 14. Dr. Wayne E. Peters, Mary Beck, and A. Richard Turner, 1971 (Photo: Rother Studio)

Fig. 15. Bob Kingsley and Adele Pierce on the road with the Friends, mid-1990s

Succeeding Betty Fishman as Chair were Mrs. William Le Baron (Mary) Beck, Dr. Wayne Peters, a popular local physician, and artist Mrs. Francis (Phyllis) Demong P'66. (Fig. 14 and Fig. 34.)

Offering an additional level of support for the Friends was its advisory committee, comprised of alumni, friends of the College, and professional colleagues. Among these were R. Dike Blair, who founded and owned the Middlebury Book Shop; Thomas W. Leavitt '51, then director of the Herbert F. Johnson Museum of Art, Cornell University, Ithaca, New York; New York art dealer Robert C. Graham, Jr. '63; painter Alan Gussow '52; recently retired faculty member and artist Arthur K. D. Healy; Julie Johnson Kidd '67; Emmy Lapham, P'70 and widow of former College Trustee Frederick W. Lapham, Jr. '43; painter and art historian Robert Reiff, of the Middlebury College Department of Fine Arts;

George Seybolt P'72, P'77, P'80; and Elsie Youngman P'64 and wife of College trustee William S. Youngman. One of the members of that first advisory committee was Robert Kingsley, who became chair of the Friends in 1974 and continues to serve actively today— as past Chair—on the board. (Fig. 15)

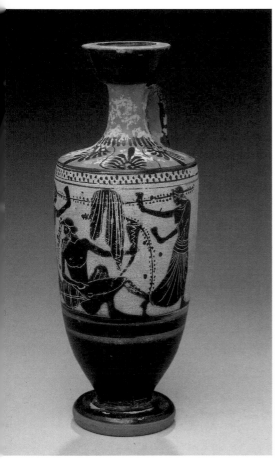

Fig. 16. *Lekythos*, Greek, late 6th century B.C.E., terracotta, h. 9 inches. Purchase with funds provided by the Friends of Art, 1969.019 (Photo: Tad Merrick)

To anyone familiar with the Friends of Art organization and with the history of Middlebury—both town and gown—these names will be instantly recognizable. And we shall have occasion to return to them, for though not all of them are still with us, forty years down the road the vital legacies associated with these family names continue to benefit the College and, in particular, its Museum of Art.

In June 1969 the Friends made their first gift of art to the collection: an Attic lekythos, or container for oil, decorated with dancers and other Dionysian figures. (Fig. 16) Indeed, a tip of the hat to Dionysus seems appropriate, since a little libation has often figured in Friends' get-togethers over the years. Early on, members brought their own hors d'oeuvres and drinks to share with one another. They met often, since exhibitions changed monthly in these years.

One of the most enduring of the Friends' activities has been their annual Purchase Party (Fig. 17), which remains a centerpiece of their programming and their mission. The first of these gatherings took place in June 1970 in the inviting atrium of the new Johnson Memorial Building. Combining a potluck supper, cocktail party, and dance, it was a festive occasion for which the community turned out elegantly dressed and ready to celebrate. In addition to being presented with fine refreshments and musical entertainment, the Friends were given an opportunity to survey several objects on loan from New York art dealers, and they would then determine by popular vote how to expend their accumulated dues. Turner recalls that in the early days there were spirited arguments between proponents favoring one acquisition and those with a decided preference for another.

Fig. 17. Purchase Party in the atrium of the Christian A. Johnson Memorial Building, June 16, 1979 (Photo: Erik Borg)

Fig. 18. Hiram Powers, *Bust of Greek Slave,* c. 1850-73, marble, 24½ × 16 × 7½ inches. Gift of the Friends of Art and the Salomon-Hutzler Foundation, 1970.006 (Photo: Tad Merrick)

At times these exchanges became quite heated, even raucous. But the upshot was that on at least one occasion, the "losing" side raised monies of its own, which would allow the Friends to purchase a second preferred piece as well. Such improvisatory developments kept the majority of voters—as well as a number of the art dealers who had made works available for short-term loan—quite happy.

Martha Lapham recalls that the Purchase Party was *the* social event of the season in Middlebury and the surrounding area. The party often coincided with openings of loan exhibitions at the Gallery and lenders from all over the state would come with their entourages to see what was on view. "No one was exhibiting art the way Middlebury was then," Lapham recalls. The shows drew viewers from far and wide—and the Purchase Parties were gala occasions for them all.[11]

For the Purchase Party that first year, Richard Wunder—a Friend of Art who was also an eminent scholar and author of a monograph on the nineteenth-century Vermont sculptor Hiram Powers—presented that artist's *Bust of a Greek Slave* for possible acquisition. (Fig. 18) The work was chosen by the Friends as its purchase for that year, and it has gone on to become the inspiration for the addition of numerous other sculptural busts—by artists such as Sir Jacob Epstein, Alexandre Falguière, François Rude, and Jean-Baptiste Carpeaux. From the outset Turner promulgated the idea that a collection should include works from different periods that would reward close comparison. That, he believed, was the value of the individual art object in the art historical curriculum, for it gave students the opportunity to comprehend, on the basis of close inspection and detailed analysis, the wide range of expression achieved by distinct styles, as well as the effects produced by variations in handling, composition, and materials.

Turner recalled in a recent telephone conversation that "he knew it would take thirty years to build a collection, and in the end that it would come about primarily through gifts from donors and their estates." As is evident in the exhibition this publication accompanies, the acquisitions purchased with membership dues over the last forty years include a very high percentage of what is currently on view continuously in the Museum's galleries. And if one were to add to these works those acquired with endowed funds contributed by Friends of Art, that list would encompass a significant portion of the entire collection.[12]

Although it has undergone numerous alterations since its inception in June 1970, the Purchase Party continues to figure prominently in the Friends' annual program of events. David Bumbeck, who directed the gallery between 1972 and 1985, and John Hunisak and Glenn Andres, who joined the Art Department in the fall of 1970, recall that by tradition the College's art faculty always selected the works presented for possible acquisition. In the early days, two members of the department would routinely drive to New

Fig. 19. Jean-Alexandre-Joseph Falguière, *Bust of Diana,* 1880s, bronze, 17¾ × 18½ × 15 inches. Purchase with funds provided by the Friends of Art Acquisition Fund, 1979.021 (Photo: Erik Borg)

Alumni Center. The sit-down dinner was now catered by the College, and the meal included the cost of wine and spirits—and service by wait staff. As late as 1983, local musician Dick Forman and his jazz ensemble provided dance music in the new venue, and though the dancing is now but a memory, the Purchase Party continues to flourish.[15] Economic conditions have required some changes of format, and the faculty presentations now are generally computer produced—that is, they

Fig. 20. Robert Reiff at the annual Purchase Party, 1971 (Photo: Rother Studio)

York and return to Vermont with three (or occasionally four) works of art in the trunk of a car. After the presentations and the voting, two (or occasionally three) of the works would be taken back to their lenders. Hunisak says that the Falguière *Bust of Diana* (acquired in 1979) was the last work he can recall delivering to Middlebury "wrapped in a blanket."[13] (Fig. 19)

When the Purchase Party took place in the Johnson Building atrium, the works for selection would be on view for the Friends, drinks and hors d'oeuvres in hand, to inspect at close range. It was not unusual for one of the faculty members to stand nearby, cheerfully exhorting Friends to vote for his particular choice. (Figs. 20–21) These parties would regularly draw as many as two hundred participants.[14]

In 1982 the purchase party moved from the Johnson Building to the College's Kirk

Fig. 21. David Bumbeck at the annual Purchase Party, 1973 (Photo: Rother Studio)

Fig. 22. Peter Walton, Gloria Offray, and Walter Brooker at *Ten Years of Friendship* exhibition, 1979 (Photo: Erik Borg)

Fig. 23. Connie and David Bumbeck with Richard Wunder at the exhibition *Architectural, Ornament, Landscape and Figure Drawings* from Wunder's collection, 1975 (Photo: Rother Studio)

feature digital reproductions of the works offered for consideration. The cost of borrowing, shipping, and insuring art these days prohibits the somewhat risky transport methods taken for granted previously. And, as Turner reflects, the relative prices for acquisitions circa 1970 will never be seen again, which imposes further limitations on continuing the more informal practices of the past.

In the group's early years, before the bylaws of the Friends of Art were adopted in the early 1970s, the Fine Arts Department, College administration, and community leadership shared the responsibility for raising dues, maintaining the regularly scheduled exhibition openings, installing exhibitions, and increasing the number of members. Professor Turner himself contacted generous donors, with the enthusiastic assistance of President and Mrs. Armstrong and Vice President and Mrs. Walter Brooker. From the start, however, College treasurer Carroll Rikert, Jr. sounded an enduring caveat: Only those potential donors "not already attracted to the College's other activities" would be solicited, so that the ongoing College business of fund-raising would be left unhampered.[16]

Thanks to the excitement and creative energy aroused in the community by the opening of the Johnson Building, with its music studios, art studios, classrooms, and gallery spaces, the Friends' membership rapidly expanded. Alumni joined local members, Vermonters from beyond Addison County gave generous gifts, and more community residents came to the fore of the leadership. In these circumstances it was not uncommon for the works on view in exhibitions to be loaned by members themselves, installed with help from other members, and greeted with interest month after month in the sequence of regular exhibition openings. (Figs. 22–25)

In the 1972–73 *Annual Report* of the Johnson Gallery, for example, the impressive two-page spread listing more than one hundred lenders of works of art for the year replaces (perhaps because it overlaps so completely) a list of the membership itself. The 1972 summer exhibition, organized by a committee of Friends headed by Dr. George Gallenkamp (1975 chair of the Friends), was *Middlebury Friends of Art Collects: Portraits, Landscapes and Sculpture*. The December exhibition of images of the Madonna and Child was organized by Professor A. Richard Turner and Mrs. Francis Demong, who chaired the group in 1972–73. In the following spring the exhibition *Middlebury Collects*, with loans from alumni, relatives, and trustees of the College, was organized by Mrs. Carol [Armstrong] Tall, assistant curator and Friend of Art; and a

Fig. 24. Installation of the 1974 exhibition *Quilts and Weathervanes* (Photo: Erik Borg)

February exhibition of early American clocks, *The Works of Time,* was organized by students—the outcome of a winter-term course co-taught by visiting art historian Alan Stone and economics professor Michael Claudon.

Under Turner's direction in its first year of operation, the Johnson Gallery showed primarily contemporary art. A loan exhibition of *Picasso Prints* led off, followed by recent works by contemporary artist and Princeton professor of art George Ortman. That artist's *The New Diamond* (1966), the first acquisition of 1969, had been exhibited at the Whitney Museum of American Art in its 1967 annual exhibition *American Art of the Twentieth Century.*[17] Its acquisition was supported by Mr. and Mrs. Frank Taplin (parents of David Taplin '72), who lived in Princeton and also had a home in southern Vermont. Ortman's structured images employed both canvas and wood in a mode very much of the moment, when many artists were building shaped canvases. His work was championed by no less an authority on contemporary art than Donald Judd, whose art criticism was as highly regarded as his minimalist constructions of the day. Upon the opening of the exhibition in Middlebury, Turner made a fifteen-minute appearance on statewide television to discuss Ortman's work.[18]

Fig. 25. Friends Peter Langrock and Deanne Wolff at reception for the exhibition *Quilts and Weathervanes,* 1974 (Photo: Erik Borg)

The New Diamond was composed of geometrically discrete elements in a symmetrical arrangement that perfectly suited its position at the central entrance to the Johnson Memorial Building, where it hung for several decades before its move, with the art collection as a whole, to the Hardy Holzmann Pfeiffer designed Center for the Arts in 1992. The work was most recently on public view in the summer 2007 museum exhibition *Modern Times,* organized by acting director of the museum Glenn Andres, chief curator Emmie Donadio, and Ondaatje Graduate Intern Sarah McCague '06, with assistance from museum intern Aglaya Glebova '07.

Among the papers of President Armstrong is a letter that described the import of the appearance on the Middlebury campus of such contemporary works of art. Thanking high profile New York art dealer Howard Wise for the loan of the painting, President Armstrong wrote:

The opening on Friday night was enormously successful in bringing town and gown together. The presence of contemporary art of this high quality is a truly important step in building the sort of art program to which we aspire. It is only with assistance from the outside such as you have provided that institutions in a rural location such as ours can develop a strong interest in the arts.[19] (Fig. 26)

Later on in that first academic year of operation the Johnson Gallery showed additional works by contemporary artists. Photographs by Frank Gohlke P'13, who would soon become an exemplar of the understated, undramatic style of landscape imagery labeled The New Topographics, were placed on view. Gohlke's wife was at the time a member of the English department, and the images he showed were shot in Cornwall, where the couple then resided. He maintained a darkroom on the top floor of the Lazarus Building (now the National Bank of Middlebury).[20]

Following Gohlke's photographs was a retrospective exhibition of works by Öyvind Fahlström, a Swedish artist who exhibited at the Sidney Janis Gallery, in New York. Like Howard Wise, whose roster of artists included pioneers like Nam June Paik and Charlotte Moorman (among the first to use television sets in their works of the 1960s), Sidney Janis was showing some of the most prominent artists of the day. Fahlström had exhibited there early in the decade with Robert Rauschenberg and Jasper Johns, in a

Fig. 26. President Armstrong (center) in the George Ortman exhibition, 1969

provocative group show of "the new realism" (a style soon to become widely known as Pop Art). The Fahlström exhibition originated at the Museum of Modern Art, New York, and after it was shown there it traveled to six college art museums.[21] Contemporary sculpture by Jean Saidenberg, on loan from James Graham & Sons in New York, formed another installation that year. A member of the advisory board of the Friends of Art, Robert C. Graham, Jr. later became president of that prominent New York gallery, which was established in the mid-nineteenth century and was one of the first to represent American modernist artists.

Graham would go on to serve as College trustee between 1992 and 2007, a position in which he was also called upon to become a member of the trustees' building committee during the College's most active construction period of the past century. A founding member of the Committee on Art in Public Places (CAPP) at Middlebury (from 1994 to the present) and of the College's Arts Council (established in 1998 to support arts programming across the curriculum), Graham remains an extraordinarily generous benefactor of the museum and the College generally—and a most valued adviser to the museum staff.

Drawing on the talents of the Friends' advisory committee—and keeping local community spirit alive—the remainder of the exhibitions during that first year of the group's existence included paintings by faculty members Robert Reiff and Bruce Muirhead, 1969 student works, and contemporary sculpture by Middlebury professor of classics William Harris. It was evident that in its initial year of programming—and before the establishment of a sizable permanent collection—the community Turner had galvanized embraced the opportunity to bring contemporary art to rural Vermont.

In his first two years as chair of the Fine Arts Department and director of the gallery, Turner launched a vital program of donor cultivation, community inclusion, and enthusiastic administrative support, and during that time the Johnson Gallery added more than 120 works to the permanent collection of the College, many of them now familiar to visitors of the Museum. Among the works that entered the collection within a year or two of its inauguration are an eighteenth-century lindenwood South German Madonna, Hans von Aachen's *Judith with the Head of Holofernes,* the Spanish sixteenth-century alabaster carving of *The Entombment*, an anonymous Italian seventeenth-century painting of *Saint Sebastian*, Hiram Power's *Bust of a Greek Slave*, and the *River Landscape* by a follower of Jan van Goyen. Mr. Egidio Moresi made a large gift of 111 etchings by Luigi Lucioni to the collection in 1970; these formed the basis of the 2009 summer museum exhibition organized by director of the museum Richard H. Saunders: *Pastoral Vermont: The Paintings and Etchings of Luigi Lucioni.*[22]

By 1971 Turner had moved on to become a member of President Armstrong's central administration, where he served as dean of faculty at the College.[23] Although he relinquished the position of director of the Johnson Gallery to David Bumbeck in 1972, Turner continued to maintain oversight of the newly launched institution and facility. As dean he described his vision for the gallery in a 1973 memo to the president that was intended to counter a somewhat narrow and essentially utilitarian view of the value of the Johnson Gallery collection then held by some. Written in his characteristically blunt, no-nonsense prose, the memo represents the far-sighted vision of the founder of our enterprise:

THE PURPOSE OF AN ART COLLECTION

The Gallery is a College and Community resource not an adjunct to the Art Department. It is a confirmation, the most tangible one along with the library that we possess, of our abiding respect for the traditions upon which our civilization is built. Further, it holds before our students our concern with possibly the most mysterious of man's abiding activities, a concern that honors those movements of the human spirit which are largely inaccessible to rational inquiry. I . . . am discomforted when colleagues on occasion imply that an art collection is the visual aids division of the Department of Art.

THE SHAPE OF THE COLLECTION

From the beginning we have tried to put the silence of the object before the words of the teacher, and have tried to acquire objects which are distinguished in quality, and have considered only secondarily the period or place from which they came. . . . Our approach, then, is eclectic, our premise quality. . . . Eventually we will specialize in one or two areas, not chosen primarily on the historical specialities of the faculty, but simply in the realization that there is a very real need to assemble closely related objects so that a student may make subtle discriminations of a sort not possible with widely diverse works of art. I would see us moving into this phase within four or five years.[24]

Succeeding Turner as director of the gallery, David Bumbeck had joined the Fine Arts Department, which included both studio artists and art historians, in 1968. (In 1970 the Department of Fine Arts became officially known as the Art Department. In 1997, it was succeeded by the Program in Studio Art and the Department of History of Art and Architecture—two separate majors and lines of study.) A consummate printmaker who has gone on in recent years—since his 2002 retirement from the College—to expand his practice and to make both sculptures and paintings, Bumbeck taught a full complement of studio classes, primarily in life drawing and printmaking, while also managing the gallery program. (The Johnson Memorial Gallery mounted a retrospective exhibition *David Bumbeck: Prints* in 1989. On the occasion of his retirement, the exhibition *David Bumbeck: Figures of the Imagination,* which also included his sculpture, was presented at the Museum.)

Fig. 27. Frances Prickitt and Barbara Andres at the annual Purchase Party, 1994 (Photo: Erik Borg)

As had been the case in the past, the staff support for the gallery drew entirely upon the Art Department. With the untiring and enthusiastic administrative assistance of department secretaries Jane Fiske and Frances Prickitt, Bumbeck orchestrated the efforts of community Friends of Art members and student volunteers in running the gallery. (Fig. 27) The collection grew from fewer than 200 works to more than 850 under his guidance. In these years the preponderance of acquisitions was in the area of works of art on paper—prints and photographs, in particular. Friends' gifts in this period—between 1972 and 1985—reflect a stepped-up pace, numbering some thirty-six.

The exhibitions Bumbeck mounted in the Johnson Gallery and the acquisitions made under his leadership reflect the catholicity of his taste and his astute and intimate knowledge of printmaking. Indeed, the most comprehensive acquisition of the mid-seventies was an impressive gathering of works by living American artists, which was acquired by the Friends through their fund-raising efforts to meet a $10,000 matching grant from the National Endowment for the Arts. This ambitious project was initiated by Professor Robert Reiff, and to insure its success the Friends pulled out all the stops.[25] Enlisting the College development office, they were able to hire students to aid in the comprehensive fund-raising effort. Among those involved were two student Friends of Art: Philip Koether '78, and Paul Rankin '76, who while

a student was an active member of the executive committee of the group.

While Bumbeck planned the exhibitions, mounted the installations in the gallery, and also served as treasurer on the executive board of the Friends, the entire Art Department was actively engaged in the development of the collection and its related programs. From the inauguration of the Friends group in 1969, professor of art Robert Reiff, an art historian who was also a highly accomplished painter, had urged the acquisition of Asian art, finding works of quality that complemented his teaching in that area. New faculty members brought to Middlebury by Turner provided invaluable assistance as well. Glenn Andres, an architect and architectural historian with a Princeton Ph.D. who arrived in the fall of 1970, mounted the exhibition *Art Nouveau* with his winter-term students in 1972. The exhibition was described in the 1972–73 *Annual Report* of the Johnson Gallery as "the first historical gallery show" to be installed in the facility. Andres has continued to play an active role in building the collection and contributing to exhibitions in the course of his 40-year career at Middlebury. He recently served as Director of the Arts and has been a leader in the development of the College's outstanding program in Architectural Studies. (Fig. 28)

Fig. 28. Helen Reiff and Glenn Andres at the annual Purchase Party, 1994 (Photo: Erik Borg)

Instructor in Art Charles Colbert, a member of the department from 1975 to 1979, organized an exhibition with his students in 1978 that put on view—and interpreted—selections from the voluminous collections of works of art on paper coming to the College from alumni donors: *Recent Acquisitions: The John Hull Brown '43 and Alice Cooke Brown '35 Collection of Prints and Drawings* included 100 prints from this major gift to the gallery.[26] In the 1976 *Annual Report*—which showed the largest growth of the collection since its founding—the director thanked Helen C. Prageman '23, who donated 140 prints by noted American artists.

Nineteenth-century sculpture, following the 1970 Friends' gift of Hiram Powers's *Bust of a Greek Slave,* became a focus of the collection in this period. Richard Wunder (who had presented the Powers bust as a possible acquisition at the Friends' first Purchase Party) remained actively engaged with the group until his departure from Vermont in 1978. Professor John M. Hunisak, a graduate of Williams College with a Ph.D. from the Institute of Fine Arts at New York University, who had joined the faculty with Andres in 1970, was a scholar of nineteenth-century sculpture. (Fig. 29) He championed acquisition of first-rate bronzes by such artists as Rude and Falguière and, eventually, Jules Dalou, who had been the subject of his doctoral thesis.[27] While the scholarly background of the faculty figured significantly in the growth of the collection, in these years the energetic sponsorship of the Friends of Art and their administrative partners Walter Brooker and President Armstrong—and later president Olin Robison, who succeeded Armstrong in 1975—continued to generate essential community support.

Among the many generous donors to the Gallery in these years Bumbeck recalls, in particular, Valtin Lust and Walter Cerf.[28] (Figs. 30–31) In his later years Cerf would bequeath to the College, in addition to numerous works of art, a considerable endowment for art acquisition, for a professorial chair, and for the naming of a gallery specifically intended for European art (the Cerf Gallery of the Museum).

Fig. 29. John Hunisak in exhibition *Rodin in His Own Words*, 2004 (Photo: Jonathan Blake)

Another early—and lasting—benefactor to the collection was George Seybolt, who joined the College community when his daughter Reva matriculated in 1968. Recently retired at that time from the presidency of the board of the Boston Museum of Fine Arts, Seybolt became a founding member of the advisory committee of the Friends. Three of his four children would attend the College, and in October 1982 he and his wife, Hortense (known affectionately to her many friends as Diddy), loaned the Johnson Gallery a number of works that comprised an exhibition called simply *The Seybolt Collection.* (Fig. 32) There are at this point three endowments that carry the names of the Seybolt children Reva B. Seybolt '72, G. Crossan Seybolt '77, and Calvert H. (Ace) Seybolt '80. Seybolt funds have made possible the addition of numerous nineteenth-century sculptures as well as photography and, with the help of Reva, the exceptionally fine group of works by living American artists acquired in 1976 with Friends' matching funds. In addition to establishing an endowment, Crossan has also served actively since 1998 on the College's Arts Council. His daughter is a member of the Middlebury Class of 2011.

Frederick (Rick) W. Lapham III '70, together with his wife, Martha, also took on an

Fig. 30. Claude Offray, Eleanor Berry, and Valtin Lust, 1986 (Photo: Erik Borg)

Fig. 32. Diddy Seybolt, G. Crossan Seybolt '77, David Bumbeck, Calvert H. Seybolt '80, George Seybolt, and John Hunisak, 1982 (Photo: Erik Borg)

Fig. 31. Betty Fishman and Walter Cerf, Purchase Party, 1988 (Photo: Erik Borg)

increasingly active role in Friends projects in these years. Lapham's mother had served on the first Friends of Art executive committee, and family friend Alice Dibble had been a driving force in the inaugural years of Friends' activity. The Laphams and Dibble assembled *Quilts and Weathervanes,* a highly regarded and extremely well-attended 1974 exhibition for the Johnson Gallery. (Figs. 24–25) Lapham also launched the Friends of Art program of visits to art sites, shepherding the group to the Adirondack Museum and to the Hyde Collection, in Glens Falls, New York. After such initial ventures, visits to Boston and Montreal, as well as to other art-worthy venues, became a Friends' continuing tradition. In 1978, when he was chair of the group, Lapham organized *Vermont Folk Art,* another highly popular exhibition. In the installation

of this show, as Martha recalls, the curator—with the help of his friends—had to wrestle an exceedingly heavy wooden buffalo into place in the gallery.[29] (Fig. 33)

The Laphams continue to provide generous philanthropic assistance to what has now become the Museum of Art. Originally supplying art loans and muscle, as well as ongoing support for the director's activities, the Laphams subsequently established an endowment that has facilitated numerous acquisitions—almost as many as their outright gifts to the collection. From the Friends, Rick has gone on to chair the College's Arts Council since its founding in 1998. In recognition of her generosity to the entire Addison County arts community Martha Lapham received the Friends of Art 2001 Award as a Benefactor of the Visual Arts, and she continues to assist the Museum in its community relations efforts as well as in its exhibition activities.

Gathering momentum from their far-flung generous founders and alumni, the Friends of Art continued to thrive as a community group through the 1970s and '80s. With his ebullient wife, Connie, Bumbeck attended all the Friends openings, Purchase Parties, and special events. The photographic record shows the couple regularly among other dapper and elegantly attired glitterati—at openings of handsome installations of American folk art, European sculpture, painting, prints, and Asian artifacts. (Figs. 13, 23) Among the

Fig. 33. Rick Lapham in the exhibition *Vermont Folk Art*, 1978 (Photo: Erik Borg)

Fig. 34. Mary Beck and Phyllis Demong at the annual Purchase Party, 1971 (Photo: Rother Studio)

Fig. 35. Sydney McCartney, Adele Pierce, Bob Kingsley at the annual Purchase Party, 1985 (Photo: Erik Borg)

Fig. 36. Marjory Cady and Irene Thompson at the annual Purchase Party, 1994 (Photo: Erik Borg)

Fig. 37. Betty Stewart and Friend at the annual Purchase Party, 1993 (Photo: Benjamin Garver '89)

memorable artists that Bumbeck and his faculty colleagues brought to visit the campus in these years—to address the Friends and the wider College community—were Bauhaus alumnus Hannes Beckmann (who taught at Dartmouth and Yale), internationally acclaimed fiber artist Sheila Hicks P'81, and the distinguished American abstract painter Jack Tworkov, who had chaired the Art Department at Yale in the 1960s.

Fig. 38. Installation view of the exhibition *The Christ and the Bodhisattva*, 1984 (Photo: Erik Borg)

What remains a particularly high point of these years, as Bumbeck recollects them, is the visit of His Holiness the 14th Dalai Lama, Tenzin Gyatso, on the occasion of the extraordinary 1984 exhibition *The Christ and the Bodhisattva*. (Fig. 38) Organized by the gallery in active collaboration with professors of religion Steven C. Rockefeller and Donald S. Lopez, Jr., the exhibition included loans from major private and public collections. The demands of the installation required Bumbeck's closest attention for an entire summer.[30] The exhibition and the visit of His Holiness brought many hundreds, if not thousands, of visitors to the gallery that fall. A 1991 sequel called *Spirit and Nature: Visions of Interdependence,* organized by Rockefeller and Professor John C. Elder, again brought His Holiness to campus, accompanied this time by other representatives from the world's major religions. (Fig. 39)

Although the Friends' ambitious program for the art education of local school children was left behind for a time after its initial success—a consequence of reordered priorities—the art education of Middlebury College students was increasing in intensity in the energizing environment of the new

facility and its distinguished faculty. Eminent alumni in the visual arts from the first decade of the Gallery's existence include the George D. Widener Director and CEO of the Philadelphia Museum of Art Timothy Rub '74, director of New York's New Museum Lisa Phillips '75, artist and independent curator Robert Gober '76, artist Steve Miller '74, and architects Philip Koether '78 and Townsend Anderson '77, among many others. In their own account of this heady time in the Christian A. Johnson Memorial Building, alumni

Fig. 39. His Holiness the 14th Dalai Lama of Tibet, Professor Seyyed Hossein Nasr, The Venerable Thupten Jinpa, and Professor Steven C. Rockefeller examine a Torah mantle in the exhibition *Spirit and Nature Visions of Interdependence*, 1991 (Photo: Erik Borg)

who were on campus at that moment testify to the ways in which the synergy of studio artists and historians of art created a richly productive, even feverish creative atmosphere. Conceptual artist Haim Steinbach, photographer Nancy Shaver, sculptor Alex Markhoff, and his successor Alex McFarlane brought a decidedly abstract, theoretical viewpoint—and a lively polemical temperament—to discussions about art. The collection in these years—including the gifts of the Friends on view—exemplifies a decided interest in geometric abstraction and art as the embodiment of ideas.

Midway through the decade, Olin Robison succeeded James Armstrong as president of the College. (Fig. 40) Continuing the collegial and community spirit established by the Armstrongs, the president's wife, Sylvia, trained as an historian, made her presence on the campus felt in a number of ways. Through her systematic survey of the campus art collection and a publication on the College's Louis XVI Salon (formerly housed in le Château), she made significant contributions to the documentation of Middlebury's holdings.[31]

For its part, the Art Department made it a priority to hire student assistants for a number of initiatives in these years. In addition to paying their Friends' yearly dues, the students contributed their energies to projects that required more than financial support. The *Annual Reports* of these years include numerous well-informed and finely crafted entries written by Middlebury students about the annual acquisitions. Not surprisingly, many of these undergraduate authors went on to careers in the arts. Among them are Koether '78, who wrote about Chuck Close's *Self Portrait* (Cat. No. 35), and Paul Rankin '76, who discussed another self portrait in the collection. A sculptor himself, John Townsend '77 contributed an impressively authoritative account of the 1976 George Rickey kinetic sculpture *Two Open Rectangles, Excentric, Variation VI,* sited before the Johnson Building. And Anne Havinga '80, who wrote about Rodin, has gone on to become curator of photography at the Boston Museum of Fine Arts.

Fig. 40. Olin Robison and Professor Emeritus of French Stephen Freeman, 1975 (Photo: Erik Borg)

The legacy of the first decades of the Gallery's existence—when departmental, College, and community ambitions overlapped and reinforced one another—continues today to affect the life of the visual arts on campus. Shortly after her graduation from Middlebury, Megan Battey '79 joined the Art Department staff. She has continued to offer indispensable support, overseeing the operation of what used to be a "slide collection" and is now a sophisticated digital resource for the entire College faculty. Later Middlebury alumni who have served both the gallery and the Museum include Friends of Art and former staff members Monica Carroll McCabe '86 and JoAnn Keeler '89, and current operations manager Douglas Perkins '94. Since 1992, when the Museum moved into the College's Center for the Arts, scores of students have received museum internship training as docents, curatorial and registrarial assistants, and preparators. The Friends have participated in many of these activities as well.

In earlier decades, before the arrival of a designated professional staff to care for the collection, the Friends and the Art Department pulled together, paving the way for the specialized information systems and management tools of the future. Looking back, both Turner and Bumbeck warmly recall the generosity and hard work of the Art Department staff and faculty as well as Friends who volunteered in the full spectrum of activities, devoting their energies to make possible a wide-ranging calendar of events.

Before he arrived at Middlebury, President Robison had been the provost at Bowdoin College, where he was instrumental in the construction of a new Visual Arts Center. He was to bring an even larger project—the Center for the Arts—to successful fruition at Middlebury before stepping down as President in 1990.

In 1985, embarking on a new era, the College hired its first museum professional, Richard H. Saunders, as director of the Christian A. Johnson Memorial Gallery. (Fig. 41) Taking over the reins of an operation younger than the student population of the College was an attractive opportunity for Saunders. An alumnus of Bowdoin College, which has maintained an art collection since 1811, and with a doctoral degree from Yale University, which launched the first university museum in America in 1832, Saunders had gained significant experience as curator of American art at the Wadsworth Atheneum, in Hartford, founded in 1842. He came to Vermont from a teaching position at the University of Texas, Austin, which boasted an art department many times larger than the one he joined at Middlebury. A scholar of portrait painting, particularly American and British, and also an alumnus of the University of Delaware Winterthur Program in Early American Culture, he set to work immediately to tend to the needs of the permanent collection, to continue the tradition of memorably installed exhibitions, and to embrace the mission and further the interests of the Friends of Art and the community at large. Part of the appeal of this broad and challenging assignment was the ambitious architectural project looming in the future: the construction of a new art

Fig. 41. Sylvia Robison with Richard and Barbara Saunders, 1986 (Photo: Erik Borg)

center to house what would become the gallery's new home.

Whereas the Art Department and the Friends had maintained what might be viewed as an informal, collaborative approach to running the gallery in the past, the appearance of a full-time director suggested a new orientation. Responsible for all programming, the director also taught the course Art Museums: Theory and Practice.[32] A priority for Saunders was the establishment of an advisory group to oversee the systematic acquisition and ongoing care of the College's permanent art collection. The members would also serve as a sounding board for establishing long-range acquisition policy. The Museum's Collections Committee, which has met regularly since 1988, reviews all works of art recommended or offered to the Museum for possible acquisition.

Within a few years of his arrival, Saunders assessed the strengths of the collection and resolved to expand the holdings in nineteenth-century sculpture, antiquities, and American photography. Such a plan would enhance areas that matched the teaching expertise of the faculty and were also still relatively affordable in the art market—which was then poised on the edge of a dramatic surge of growth and a corresponding rise in prices.

Under the leadership of the Chief Curator, the Collections Committee now is comprised of the chair of the Program in Studio Art and the chair of the Department of History of Art and Architecture, a member of the Friends of Art, and a representative from the president's staff. The first administrator to serve on this new committee was long-time Friend of Art John M. McCardell, Jr., who at the time of the committee appointment was provost of the College and who subsequently, between 1991 and 2004, served as its president. Community member and Friend of Art J. Robert Maguire, of Shoreham, has been a judicious and articulate participant in committee deliberations since its inception. The historical acumen and legal perspective of this lawyer, author, and scholar, in addition to his generosity, have been invaluable assets to the committee. (Fig. 42)

Fig. 42. J. Robert Maguire and Friends, 1980 (Photo: Erik Borg)

When the Friends group was conceived in 1969, the future was a series of blank pages, and it was not clear what story would emerge as the years passed. By the mid-eighties, in addition to regularly changing exhibitions and a cadre of Friends of Art who were on the lookout for those newly arrived in the community to join them, there was a sizable permanent art collection to manage. Numbering nearly nine hundred objects by 1985, the collection was stored floor to ceiling in two closets on either side of the former Christian A. Johnson Gallery space. Without provision for controlling the fluctuating temperatures and humidity index, the condition of a number of the works of art would be seriously compromised. And if the collection were to continue to grow, attract significant gifts, and have any hope of bringing Middlebury up to the standards maintained by any number of its New England "sister" schools (that is, the group competing for bright students and a distinguished faculty—Williams, Amherst, and Bowdoin, for example), the gallery would need more than Friends of Art to assist in its mission.

Saunders's first hire, Christine Fraioli '74, now a member of the board of the Friends of the Art Museum, served as registrar and all-around assistant to the director through 1991, and as consulting conservator and preparator for many years thereafter. Soon a gifted designer, Ken Pohlman '78, who had attended the College and ultimately completed a bachelor of fine arts degree in film at New York University, was added to the staff. Visitors to our exhibitions are well aware that he has remained integral to the operation ever since. In 1990 the current chief curator of the Museum (and author of this text) became the assistant director—charged, in addition to curatorial duties, with maintaining oversight of the Friends of Art. Assisting in that sphere of activity now are Douglas Perkins '94, administrative operations manager, who serves as treasurer of the Friends of the Art Museum, and Andrea Solomon, events and exhibitions coordinator and museum liaison for all Friends' programs and events.

Early in his directorship Saunders moved to make the gallery a part of the consortium of institutions that support and are in turn served by the Williamstown Art Conservation Center, in Williamstown, Massachusetts.[33] Regular visits and consultations with conservators of works of art on paper, paintings, and sculpture have followed, as needed, and a portion of the annual budget is set aside for ongoing collection maintenance. The hiring of Margaret Wallace as museum registrar in 1997 has further insured consistent attention to the care of the collection. Wallace has also overseen the digitization of the museum's

Fig. 43. Reverend Wilson A. Farnsworth, Class of 1848, and his family. Boston, 1867. Photograph found in private collection on deposit with the Thetford Historical Society, Thetford, VT. Reproduced with permission.

a J. Paul Getty Foundation matching grant for conservation of the first art property ever accessioned by the College: the sculptural relief from the Palace of Ashurnasirpal II at Nimrud, 759 C.E. Delivered to the campus in 1898, a gift of the Reverend Wilson Farnsworth, Class of 1848 and former missionary in Turkey (Fig. 43), this extraordinary artifact was originally located in what is now Iraq. It was cut into sections and brought overland—by camel, boat, and local means of transport—and ultimately installed in Old Chapel. In 1941 the sculpture was moved to Munroe Hall, then a new classroom building. Now requiring conservation, cleaning, and a steel support structure, the relief was to be removed from Munroe and sent to the Fogg Art Museum Conservation Laboratory at Harvard University, ultimately to be returned for reinstallation in the lobby of the new Museum. The cost of treatment and de- and re-installation, a three-year project, would be shared by the Friends of Art and the J. Paul Getty Foundation.

Virginia Faurote, a former chair of the Friends of Art, along with the current chair Margaret Keith, led the Friends' fund-raising campaign. Their committee included Ted Colwell, Harold Curtiss, Nan Lambeth, Louise Hubbard McCoy '36, and Alyse Mills.[34] The ambitious initiative was launched with a festive summer garden party at the presidential home of the Robisons, 3 South Street. Eighteen months later, on a snowy February night in 1990, the Friends gathered in Munroe Hall to celebrate the success of their fund-raising campaign.[35] (Fig. 44) And in October 1992, they reconvened in the lobby of the new Middlebury College Museum of Art, where the sculpture was permanently installed. Presented and placed in a comprehensive historical context in a well-attended public lecture (and in an essay in that year's *Annual Report*) by Dr. Samuel M. Paley, of the State University of New York, Buffalo, the relief now anchors the Museum's installation of ancient Near Eastern art.[36]

Between the launch of the Friends' fund-raising campaign and the repositioning and restoration of the Assyrian relief, the board

database and improved electronic access to it, and she has supervised the production of numerous award-winning museum publications.

The professionalization of the gallery staff has inevitably led to a lessening of the intense, hands-on involvement of Friends volunteers in every aspect of institutional operation. While they once brought their own food and drink to festive gallery openings and Purchase Parties, the College's catering department—which flourished throughout the nineties and into the new millennium (until the recent economic downturn)—relieved them for a time from those responsibilities. Organizing temporary exhibitions, which often in the past had involved curatorial input as well as loans from the private art collections of the Friends (not to mention heavy lifting and toting), now called more regularly for initiatives undertaken by the director and his faculty and staff colleagues. Soon, however, the Friends determined that they wished to return to one of their primary purposes: developing an educational outreach program to interpret the collection and make it accessible to the local community.

Before undertaking that project, however, they made another crucial contribution. In 1988, in preparation for the relocation of the art collection to the College's Center for the Arts after the completion of construction, the Friends took on the challenge of meeting of trustees of the College had endorsed the establishment of the Middlebury College Museum of Art. Transfer of the collection and relocation of the Christian A. Johnson Memorial Gallery—to become a designated space for temporary loan exhibitions in the new facility—followed. Robert C. Graham, Jr. '63; Robert P. Youngman '64, P'90, P'97; and J. Lea Hillman Simonds '69, P'93, P'97—trustees serving under presidents Olin Robison, Timothy Light, and John M. McCardell, Jr.—were among those who participated in the historic decisions that led to the transformation of the Johnson Gallery. When the Museum opened in 1992 it housed three named galleries. In addition to the Christian A. Johnson Memorial Gallery were the Overbrook Gallery, endowed by the Overbrook Foundation, and the Walter Cerf Gallery, endowed by Mr. Cerf. Through Marianne Boesky '89, the reception area was subsequently endowed as the Boesky Family Entrance Court.

As had the Christian A. Johnson Memorial Building, the new Center for the Arts facility attracted a wide public. Both newcomers to the community and returning alumni continue to find Middlebury a remarkably lively destination thanks to the impressive range of arts activities at the College. And the founding Friends, as well as new ones, have continued to donate significant works to the collection and also to establish endowments that support its growth and care. The new facility has made it possible for the first time to store the artworks in spaces that meet recommended museum standards for controlling fluctuations in temperature and humidity. With the physical plant improvements and the goal of seeking accreditation by the American Association of Museums, the arbiter of national standards and governing body of museum professionals, the director applied in 1995 for a grant from the American Association of Museums Museum Assessment Program. Receiving this grant initiated an ambitious self-study project that involved the entire staff and brought a designated museum leader to campus for on-site consultations. That leader was Middlebury alumnus Timothy Rub, who at the time was serving as director of the

Fig. 44. Nan Lambeth, Peggy Keith, and Friends at Assyrian Relief in Munroe Hall, February 1990 (Photo: Erik Borg)

Hood Museum at Dartmouth College. (Rub went on to similar positions at the Cincinnati Art Museum and the Cleveland Museum of Art before assuming the directorship of the Philadelphia Museum of Art in 2009.) Meeting with museum staff, College administrators and faculty, and Friends of the Art Museum, Rub was charged with evaluating the operation of the Museum in all of its relationships to the College and the community at large. In his official report, among other recommendations, he encouraged the Museum to develop an educational outreach plan that would enhance its presence in the larger community and also demonstrate its extraordinary value to those beyond the boundaries of the College campus.

This recommendation echoed the very principles and programs that the gallery founders, the College administration, director A. Richard Turner, and the first executive committee of the Friends of Art had endorsed at the group's inception in 1969. Subsequently the long-range planning and special projects committee of the Friends of the Art Museum, led by Rev. Lawrence C. Whittemore, Jr.—and including Harold Curtiss, who well remembered the original intent of the Friends—was formed to implement the recommendation. Also serving on this committee were Virginia Faurote, Eleanor Flandreau

Josset '51, Shirley Whitney Juneo '58, Bobbie Mankey, and Lawson Stewart. And playing an important role in the work of the committee was Bonnie McCardell, who as spouse of the College president was an ex-officio member of the Friends board and a tireless advocate for education in the broader community.[37] The committee recommended altering the Friends' bylaws to redirect the distribution of their membership funds. Henceforth two-thirds of the dues would fund a new educational outreach project, while one-third would continue to support acquisitions for the museum collection.

The board of the Friends unanimously endorsed the committee's recommendation, and the Museum soon launched its current education program. Its implementation provided the Friends, as well as Middlebury College students, with an opportunity to insure an important collaborative relationship between town and gown. Required of all docents, who were called Museum Assistants, was a commitment to a weekly training session led by the museum's newly appointed curator for education, Sandra Olivo. From her involvement in the community over many years as educator at the town's Henry Sheldon Museum, Olivo was well aware of the opportunities for collaboration that such a position afforded. In addition to launching the Museum's outreach program, Olivo soon, on behalf of all of the arts programs housed in the center, engaged the local school board and the superintendent of schools in a program called "Midd Arts." This state-funded enterprise brings local school children to performances that embrace all the arts in the facility, which in 2007 was named the Kevin P. Mahaney '85 Center for the Arts in honor of a major donor.

In the first year of its existence the Museum Assistants Program included eighteen Middlebury students and four members of the Friends of the Art Museum: Helen Freismuth, Betsy Heath Gleason '58, Ginny Hiland P'89, and Shirley Whitney Juneo '58. (Fig. 45) The success of the program was acknowledged by its local beneficiaries— schoolteachers and their pupils alike—and it garnered national foundation support within

Fig. 45. First group of Museum Assistants, 1996: l. to r. rear row: Jonathan Ferrari '97, Amy Flanders '97, Larry McDermott '99, Mari Walcutt '99; second from top: Betsy Gleason '58, Lesli Stinger '97, Molly Peppo '97; second from bottom: Tasha Farrar '97, Emily Olsc '98, Anna Foster '97; bottom: Briana Miller'96, Sandra Olivo, Ginny Hiland 'P89, Shirley Juneo '58. 1996 (Photo: Jonathan Blake)

a few years of its inception. The Arthur and Helen Baer Charitable Foundation, of St. Louis, was an early and generous source of support and encouragement. The Baer Foundation contributed to the operations of the educational program geared toward students from kindergarten through twelfth grade and also made a lasting gift to the collection by funding acquisition of works of art best suited to the Visual Thinking Strategies curriculum adapted by Olivo to the needs of the larger Middlebury community.[38] The Baer Family includes a number of Middlebury alumni. Among them are Rosemary Baer '34, Julius (Ted) Baer '67 and his brother Terence Baer '77, who are sons of J. Arthur Baer. Other Baer grandchildren have attended the College as well. Among these are Jeffrey Fisher '82 and Christopher Baer Fisher '09. The ongoing support of the Baer Foundation has helped the Museum education program to thrive from its inauguration into its second decade of existence. (Fig. 46)

Shortly after the creation of the educational outreach program, another Friends initiative was launched. In 1998, in order to provide further encouragement for the appreciation of art and artists in the community, the Friends' Awards for Distinction in the Visual Arts came into being. These awards are given annually to individuals who have made outstanding contributions—either

Fig. 46. Museum Assistant Kate Lupo '10 with children in the gallery, 2007 (Photo: Jonathan Blake)

Fig. 47. Sixth Grade Arts Award recipient Florence Howell with her parents, Friends' Annual Meeting, 2001 (Photo: Jonathan Blake)

Fig. 48. Middlebury College Senior Arts Award recipient Andrew Lynch '06 with President Emeritus and Mrs. John M. McCardell, Jr., 2006 (Photo: Jonathan Blake)

through exceptional creative achievement or through vital support of the visual arts in Addison County. The categories for recipients, who are nominated by community members, include Middlebury College seniors; high school seniors; eighth-grade students; sixth-grade students; teachers in public or private schools; professional or amateur artists, craftspersons, or teachers; and arts benefactors, volunteers, or organizations. Awards are not always given in each of these categories every year, but since 1998 the distinction has meant a great deal to many people. Each year's recipients are recognized by the Friends at their annual meeting and supper. To date, some eighty-two awardees have received a certificate designed by William R. (Woody) Jackson '70, and a significant number of the younger recipients, who also receive a token honorarium, have gone on to pursue their interest in art at college, as well as in art schools, graduate study, and professional careers in the arts. (Figs. 47–48)

In 2005, through the extraordinary philanthropy of Robert P. and Barbara P. Youngman, the Museum designated one of its rooms as the Robert F. Reiff Gallery, a space dedicated specifically to the permanent display of Asian art. (Fig. 49) The gallery has enhanced the presentation of works on continuous view at the Museum, broadening the range and elevating the quality of the overall collection in a way that would have delighted Robert Reiff. Youngman, whose mother, Elsie, had served on the first advisory committee of the

Friends of Art and whose father, Willam S. Youngman, served on the College's Board of Trustees from 1963 to 1977, was himself chair of the Board of Trustees from 1993 through 1996. As a student, he had been introduced to the study of Asian art—in an unforgettably vivid and tangible manner—by Professor Robert Reiff. It was Reiff's custom to circulate objects of inquiry hand-to-hand among the students in his classroom. Youngman, who would spend many years in southeast Asia following graduation from Middlebury, acquired a love and a literal feel for objects of art in Reiff's classroom. In addition to the Gallery space dedicated to his teacher, the Youngmans endowed a position to be shared equally between the Museum and the Department of History of Art and Architecture: the Robert P. Youngman Curator of Asian Art. This was the

Fig. 49. Barbara and Robert Youngman in the Robert F. Reiff Gallery, 2005 (Photo: Jonathan Blake)

first—and, to date, the single—named curatorial position at the Museum.

Arriving at the College in 2003 as the first scholar to hold the Youngman position, Colin Mackenzie soon made an indelible mark on the Museum's outstanding collections. Educated in London, with teaching and curatorial experience at Yale University and a noteworthy record of curatorial accomplishment at the Asia Society in New York, he augmented the existing Asian artifacts with significant acquisitions, amplifying the range and depth of the Museum's holdings. Under his watch and at his hearty recommendation at their 2004 Purchase Party, the Friends selected a magnificent Wei Dynasty *Caparisoned Horse* for acquisition. (Frontispiece, Cat. No. 70)

The structure of the Youngman curatorship made possible the simultaneous integration of the teaching of Asian art and the development and growth of the Asian collection. Mackenzie's students were involved directly in research on the permanent collection. Contributing their own scholarly efforts in addition to Mackenzie's public presentations, they had opportunities to speak about their

research and wrote label texts that introduced Asian ceramics, in particular, to the Museum public. The burgeoning collection has been extremely well regarded by both campus and community visitors, complementing the College's highly regarded Schools of Chinese and Japanese and its distinguished academic departments in those languages as well as in religion and East Asian and International Studies.

Mackenzie recently moved on to a prestigious curatorial position at the Nelson-Atkins Museum of Art, in Kansas City, which has one of the most extensive Asian collections in the country, and we await the appointment of a worthy successor. A highly visible and enduring accomplishment, this joint project of the Museum, the College faculty, and the Youngmans—true Friends of Art—has been a gift to the community of incalculable value. Its benefits will only become more evident in future years.

The appointment of a curator for Asian art stimulated additional staff changes at the Museum. Formerly associate director, Emmie Donadio was subsequently named chief curator. Other areas of the collection were enhanced as Professor of History of Art and Architecture Pieter Broucke was designated associate curator of ancient art. (Fig. 50) In addition to being an architect, Broucke brought with him considerable curatorial experience gained when he worked as a graduate student in the Ancient Art Department of the Yale University Art Gallery. An active archaeologist, he also participated regularly in summer excavations at Ancient Messene, in Greece. In conjunction with a First Year Seminar Broucke taught in fall 2006, newly arrived Middlebury students were introduced to the college curriculum with an enviable opportunity to study a remarkable array of *Treasures from the Royal Tombs of Ur*. The installation of this temporary exhibition, which was on loan from the University of Pennsylvania Museum of Art, was made possible at the College with funds from the Christian A. Johnson Memorial Endeavor Foundation as well as generous support from the College's Arts Council. Among the Friends of Art who served on the Council and offered support for this extraordinary curricular enrichment were founding Friends of Art Robert P. Youngman, Robert C. Graham, Jr., and G. Crossan Seybolt. Also contributing to this effort and serving on the Arts Council at the time were alumni J. Lea Hillman Simonds '69, Anne Curtis Odom '58, P'87, Timothy Rub '74, Lisa Ackerman '82, Paul R. Provost '87, Marianne Boesky '89, and Arianna Faber Kolb '88, all of whom have maintained long-standing relations to the Museum, its staff, and the art faculty.[39]

The participants in that First Year Seminar on *Treasures of Ur* have recently become graduates of Middlebury College. Among them are several students who will be pursuing graduate study in classics and in the history of art and architecture. The Friends of the Art Museum and all of the Museum's benefactors are delighted and encouraged to see the effects of their contributions to the College realized in such immediate—and lasting— ways.

Not only compelling in the classroom, Broucke has also succeeded in persuading the Friends of the Art Museum to use their dues

Fig. 50. Professor and Associate Curator Pieter Broucke in the exhibition *Treasures from the Royal Tombs of Ur*, 2006 (Photo: Jonathan Blake)

to acquire three works of classical antiquity— in the course of only five years. [Catalogue Numbers 72, 75, and 76.] The permanent installation of antiquities at the Museum shows the splendid results of his conscientious and determined efforts.

Another area of acquisition that has been made possible by the network of connections between the Museum, the Friends of Art, and alumni of the Art Department is contemporary photography and video art. Marianne Boesky, working with director Richard Saunders, initiated a remarkable program that enables Middlebury College students—with curatorial guidance and approval by the Collections Committee—to realize their preferences for additions to the permanent collection. Since 1999, when the program commenced, the students have selected 42 works of contemporary photography and video art that have been accessioned. After only five years the acquisitions were installed as the Museum exhibition *Screened and Selected: Contemporary Photography & Video Acquisitions 1999–2005*. The mid-course installation, a project of Emmie Donadio and

Reiff Intern Phillip Bloom '05, who is now completing a Ph.D. in the history of Chinese art at Harvard University, will be followed by a second installment in the near future. Since 2006 a January term course taught by Donadio has offered students the opportunity to do extensive research in preparation for a visit to New York or Boston to see works under consideration for possible acquisition. Well informed presentations by these students to a larger group assembled for this purpose have made possible the most recent additions to the Museum collection of photography and video art. A number of these works are being shown in the Fall 2010 exhibition *Moving Images*, a joint project of the Museum and Assistant Professor of Media Studies Hope Tucker.

With a recent gift from the Foster Family Art Acquisition Fund (Family of Zachary Foster '06) earmarked specifically for contemporary art, the collection of recent art at the Museum continues to gain in stature and significance. A permanent gallery to display ongoing installations of works of art on paper and new media—including photography and video art—remains a cherished dream for the Museum, one that still awaits realization.

In 2005 the Middlebury College Museum of Art was accredited by the American Association of Museums. This designation acknowledges that it has met high standards of professionalism in its maintenance of the art collection, its distinguished educational outreach program, and the overall excellence of its exhibitions and related programming. No small element in this success story has been the continuing commitment of the Friends of the Art Museum. Vital relations with the immediate and regional community and a recognition of the cultural needs of those larger communities have defined the efforts of the Friends since the group's founding. And the membership has grown in recent years with appeals to the broader alumni population through the efforts of trustees Linda Foster Whitton '80 and David Salem '78.

The program in Studio Art and the Department of History of Art and Architecture continue to provide the Museum with student volunteers as well as loyal alumni whose activities benefit the arts on campus in general and the Museum in particular. The Arts Council membership, in addition to its chair and the members cited above, includes a wide range of more recent alumni with ties to the visual arts at the College. Among these are Kirtley Horton Cameron '95, Jean G. Fritts-Eskenazi '86, Natasha Elkon Houze '96, Sydney H. Johnston '02, Lindsay Marx '87, Charles S. Moffett '67, P'04, Sarah Ondaatje '85, Lee Findlay Potter '85, and Henry J. Simonds '97. All of these alumni have offered—and continue to provide—generous support for the Museum and the programs in the history of art and architecture and studio art. Their persistent beneficence will undoubtedly be celebrated once again by the author of the next installment of the ongoing history of the Friends of the Art Museum at Middlebury College.

Indeed, as we look back at the past forty years, it is hard to imagine achieving all that we have achieved without the good Friends who have been at our side. Those who are with us today and those whom we have every reason to believe will follow in their footsteps make us confident that a rich and vital legacy has been secured.

NOTES

1. Arthur K. D. Healy, Inaugural Exhibition brochure, p. 27.

2. Betty Fishman, telephone conversation with the author, March 15, 2010.

3. As quoted in *The Campus*, October 17, 1968. On the occasion of his address, Hoving received an honorary degree of Doctor of Letters from the College. The citation called him "collector, preserver, exhibitor, educator, [who] has made the cause of art that of all men in our day."

4. David M. Stameshkin, *The Strength of the Hills: Middlebury College, 1915–1990*. Hanover, New Hampshire: 1996, p. 129.

5. www.dictionaryofarthistorians.org/matherf.htm.

6. Letter, A. Richard Turner to Mrs. Christian A. Johnson. College Archives, A3 V-P/Dir. of Dev. 2 Corresp. Friends of Art 1967–70.

7. A. Richard Turner, *Annual Report*, 1969, p. 3.

8. Telephone conversation with the author, March 8, 2010.

9. Telephone conversation with the author.

10. John M. Hunisak, conversation with the author, May 5, 2010.

11. Conversation with the author May 14, 2010.

12. See "List of Named and Endowed Funds," page 45.

13. Conversation with the author, May 5, 2010.

14. Harold Curtiss, *Friends of Art Newsletter*, Winter 1986.

15. Harold Curtiss, *Friends of Art Newsletter*, Fall 1983.

16. College Archives, A3 V-P/Dir. of Dev. 2 Corresp. Friends of Art 1967–70.

17. A. Richard Turner, Ortman exhibition catalogue, Johnson Gallery, 1969.

18. Johnson Gallery Scrapbook, Courtesy of David Bumbeck.

19. Letter, James Armstrong to Howard Wise, February 12, 1969, College Archives, A3 Development 2.1. Office Records Johnson Gallery 1968-1969.

20. Frank Gohlke, interview with the author, March 19, 2010.

21. In addition to the Johnson Gallery at Middlebury, these were at the University of Texas; the University of Georgia; the University of Minnesota; Edinboro State [Pennsylvania]; and Sacramento State College [California]. www.fahlstrom.com/01_exhibitions_solo.asp?id=1&subid=2.

22. See the exhibition catalogue. Middlebury: Middlebury College Museum of Art, 2009.

23. In 1975 Turner was named president of Grinnell College. In 1979 he became Director of the Institute of Fine Arts at New York University and, subsequently, Dean of the Faculty of Arts and Sciences. From 1994 until his retirement from New York University in 2000 he was Paulette Goddard Professor in Arts and Humanities.

24. Letter to President Armstrong from A. Richard Turner, June 21, 1972. College Archives, A3 Development 2.2. Office Records Johnson Gallery 1970–1989.

25. David Bumbeck, "The Director's Note," Christian A. Johnson Memorial Gallery *Annual Report* for the Year 1982, np.

26. Listed in the Johnson Gallery 1978 *Annual Report* as on view from February 8 through March 25 of that year.

27. The museum now owns three sculptures by Dalou, as well as a painting by Alphonse Gaudefroy of Dalou's studio. See John M. Hunisak, "Jules Dalou at Middlebury," Middlebury College Museum of Art *Annual Report*, 2003–2004, pp. 8–19.

28. Conversation with the author, April 13, 2010.

29. Conversation with the author, May 14, 2010.

30. Conversation with the author, April 13, 2010.

31. See "Le Chateau 1925" and "Notes on Le Chateau and the Salon Louis XVI." College Archives, A 12 Middlebury College Buildings 1 A-J.

32. See the Johnson Gallery 1987 *Annual Report*, np.

33. Friends of Art *Newsletter*, Vol. 1, no. 2 [Winter/Spring 1987], np.

34. Friends of Art *Newsletter*, Vol 5, no. 2 [Fall 1990], np.

35. Connie Sophocles-Miller, "The 20th Anniversary Project," Friends of Art *Newsletter*, Vol. 5, no. 2 [Summer/Fall 1990], p. 8.

36. See Samuel M. Paley, "The Assyrian *Winged Genius* in the Middlebury College Museum of Art," The Middlebury College Museum of Art *Annual Report*, 1992, pp. 13–31.

37. Friends of the Art Museum *Newsletter*, Vol. 12, no. 1 [Fall 1997], np.

38. Visual Thinking Strategies (VTS) is a research-based teaching method developed within the past half century that is aimed particularly at grade-school children and intended through discussions of visual images to improve their critical thinking and language skills. Well suited to Museum education programs, it is in wide use throughout the U.S. For additional information see the Visual Understanding in Education website www.vtshome.org.

39. In 2003 Anne Odom, curator emerita at Hillwood, the Marjorie Merriweather Post Museum, in Washington, D.C., had served as guest curator of the notable museum exhibition *What Became of Peter's Dream? Court Culture in the Reign of Nicholas II*. Middlebury College Museum of Art, Vermont, in Association with Hillwood Museum and Gardens, Washington, D.C., 2003.

Two Scenes from the Life of Buddha, 2nd–3rd centrury, stone, 16 × 14 inches. Purchase with funds provided by the Friends of Art Acquisition Fund, 1972.002 (Photo: Ken Burris)

Friends of the Art Museum Chronology

1968

Fall. Homecoming weekend. Inauguration of Christian A. Johnson Memorial Building endowed by the Christian A. Johnson Endeavor Foundation. Professor of Fine Arts A. Richard Turner serves as first director of the Christian A. Johnson Memorial Gallery.

Turner launches a Friends group to support gallery activities, expand the permanent art collection of the College, and bring art into the community, specifically to the local school population. President James I. Armstrong, his wife, Carol, and daughter Cary A. Tall participate actively in Friends' activities with enthusiastic support of vice president Walter E. Brooker '37 and his wife, Barbara-Ann Carrick Brooker '40.

1969

Spring. First meeting of the Friends of Art conducted by chair Mrs. Samuel (Betty) Fishman. Mrs. Christian A. Johnson serves as honorary chair of the Friends.

First exhibition organized by the Friends, who also circulate original prints to local schools and offer Saturday morning art classes for elementary school children. Forty students enroll.

Publication of first *Annual Report* of the Christian A. Johnson Gallery (see Bibliography).

First gift of the Friends to the gallery is a Greek lekythos (see Fig. 16).

1970

June. First Friends of Art Purchase Party. Hiram Powers, *Bust of Greek Slave* (Cat. No. 3) selected by Friends as gift for the permanent collection.

1972

First exhibition in conjunction with the art history curriculum organized by professor Glenn Andres and his January-term class on Art Nouveau.

David Bumbeck becomes director of the gallery. Turner joins College administration as dean of faculty.

1975

Olin Robison becomes thirteenth president of the College. Sylvia Robison, as ex-officio member of the Friends, writes history of the College's Salon Louis XVI and begins to compile complete inventory of art on campus.

1978

Friends' trip program inaugurated by Chair Frederick W. Lapham III '70 with a bus tour to the Hyde Collection in Glens Falls, New York.

1982

Exhibition *The Seybolt Collection* features works from Friends of Art George and Diddy Seybolt and family.

1984

Major exhibition *The Christ and the Bodhisattva,* organized by Bumbeck and professors of religion Donald S. Lopez and Steven C. Rockefeller. The exhibition and related programs bring His Holiness Tenzin Gyatso, the fourteenth Dalai Lama of Tibet, and thousands of visitors to campus.

Friends' mimeographed *Newsletter* launched. The printed publication commences in summer 1986 (see Bibliography).

1985

Richard H. Saunders appointed first College curator and director of the Christian A. Johnson Memorial Gallery. With President Robison, Professor of History of Art Glenn Andres, and architect Malcolm Holzman, Saunders works on plan for new arts facility to house the growing collection.

1986

Saunders connects Gallery to consortium of institutions supporting the Williamstown Regional Art Conservation Laboratory and begins regular conservation of works in the collection.

1988

Establishment of five-member Collections Committee to oversee all acquisitions to the permanent collection. J. Robert Maguire represents the Friends of Art on the committee.

August. Garden Party at President Robison's residence, 3 South Street, to inaugurate Friends of Art 20th Anniversary Project: funding to conserve the College's Assyrian Relief from Palace of Ashurnasirpal II (Nimrud, 8th century B.C.E. Cat. No. 1). After conservation the sculptural relief will be installed in the lobby of the new art facility. Coordinators of fund-raising campaign are Virginia Faurote (ex-chair of Friends), Margaret Keith (current chair of Friends), Ted Colwell, Harold Curtiss, Nan Lambeth, Louise Hubbard McCoy '36, and Alyse Mills.

1990

Celebratory champagne reception marks success of Friends' fund-raising project, which is matched by a conservation grant from the J. Paul Getty Trust.

Timothy Light becomes fourteenth College president. Joy Light serves ex-officio on board of the Friends of Art.

1991

John M. McCardell, Jr., becomes fifteenth College president. Bonnie McCardell serves ex-officio on board of the Friends, assisting in launch of educational outreach program in the community.

1992

October. Inauguration of newly named Middlebury College Museum of Art in the Center for the Arts building. Christian A. Johnson Gallery continues as a space for changing exhibitions. The Overbrook Gallery and the Cerf Gallery house permanent collection.

1993

Board of Trustees of the College adopts mission statement of the Middlebury College Museum of Art and declares museum a permanent and integral part of the College.

1994

College establishes Committee on Art in Public Places [CAPP] to oversee acquisition and maintenance of public art on campus. Professor John Hunisak is chair of committee, which includes members of museum staff, College trustees, faculty, College administrative officers, and students.

1995

With goal of accreditation, Museum and Friends participate in self-study with grant from the Museum Assessment Program of the American Association of Museums. Study conducted by Timothy Rub '74.

1996

Friends change bylaws to redirect two-thirds of their membership funds toward development of a community-wide educational outreach program. One-third of dues continues to fund acquisitions for the collection.

1996–97

Sandra Olivo, newly hired curator of education, launches Museum Assistants Program. Twenty-two volunteer docents take weekly training sessions in fall and spring terms. In addition to Middlebury students, volunteers include Friends of Art Helen Freismuth, Betsy Heath Gleason '58, Virginia Hiland P'89, and Shirley Whitney Juneo '58.

1998

Spring. Friends launch Annual Arts Awards program.

September. Friends celebrate their thirtieth anniversary with champagne brunch in the Center for the Arts. Among the founders present are President Emeritus and Mrs. James I. Armstrong, Mr. and Mrs. Walter Brooker, Dr. and Mrs. A. Richard Turner, Betty Fishman, Harold Curtiss, and Bob Kingsley. President John M. McCardell, Jr. addresses the group.

2000

Bicentennial celebration of the founding of the College. The Museum mounts exhibitions *50 Years of Faculty Art* organized by associate director Emmie Donadio and *13 Alumni Artists,* co-curated by Donadio, Timothy Rub '74, Marianne Boesky '89, and James Rondeau '91. Publication *13 Alumni Artists* includes introduction by Lisa Phillips '75, essay by Avital Ronell '74, and a history of art instruction at the College. Artists included are Bill Burke '66, Peter Cole '87, Fred Cray '79, George Creamer '74, Jeremy Foss '54, Peter Gallo '81, Robert Gober '76, Valerie Hegarty '89, Peter Krashes '85, Steve Miller '73, Julia Rossman Perez '90, Susanna Harwood Rubin '89, and Julia Wachtel '78.

2002

Friends of the Art Museum and newly formed Arts Council raise funds to bring the exhibition *American Art from the Smithsonian American Art Museum* to campus.

2003

Ronald D. Liebowitz becomes sixteenth president of the College. His wife, Jessica, joins board of the Friends of the Art Museum.

2005

The museum, meeting highest standards for care of its collections and distinction of its exhibitions and programs, is accredited by the American Association of Museums.

September. Inauguration and dedication of the Robert F. Reiff Gallery, which is devoted to the ongoing exhibition of Asian art. Robert P. Youngman Curator of Asian Art Colin Mackenzie speaks at inaugural exhibition to group that includes the Youngmans, Helen Reiff, and President Liebowitz.

2006

Arts Council and Friends raise funds to bring exhibition *Treasures from the Royal Tombs of Ur* (organized by the University of Pennsylvania Museum of Archaeology and Anthropology) to campus.

2008

Arts Council raises funds to conserve fifteenth-century Florentine panel painting *Virgin and Child* by Lippo d'Andrea, which is subsequently the centerpiece of 2009 Museum exhibition *The Art of Devotion: Panel Painting in Early Renaissance Italy.*

2010

Celebratory exhibition *Friends Bearing Gifts* and this publication highlight the forty-year history of acquisitions and achievements of the Middlebury College Friends of Art and Friends of the Art Museum.

All acquisitions purchased with funds from the Friends of the Art Museum are listed on pages 47 through 61.

Friends of Art and Friends of the Art Museum
Chairs 1969–2011

1969 Betty Fishman
1970 Dr. Wayne E. Peters
1971 Mary Beck
1972–73 Phyllis Demong P'66
1974 Robert Kingsley
1975 George V. Gallenkamp
1976–77 Eleanor Benjamin Clemens Berry '32
1978–79 Frederick W. Lapham III '70
1980–81 Mildred Aubrey Monagan '35
1982–83 Harold M. Curtiss
1984–87 Virginia Faurote
1988–90 Margaret Keith

1990–91 Nan Lambeth
1992–93 Mary Jo Champlin P'95
1994–95 Nan Lambeth
1996–97 Lawson Stewart
1998–99 Bobbie Mankey
1999–2001 Rev. H. Lawrence Whittemore, Jr.
2001–2003 Virginia Perkins
2003–2004 Gary Starr
2005–2007 Nancy Ewen
2007–2009 Jacqueline Ogden English '69
2009–2011 Barbara Blodgett

Named and Endowed Acquisition and Support Funds

ELECTRA HAVEMEYER WEBB
MEMORIAL FUND (1965)
Established by Harry H. Webb '44 as a permanently endowed fund at Middlebury College in memory of Mrs. Electra Havemeyer Webb, Doctor of Humanities (Honorary). The income is to be used each year for Fine Arts Acquisitions for Middlebury College.

THE FINE ARTS ACQUISITION FUND
(1967)

THE FRIENDS OF ART ACQUISITION
FUND (1969)
Originally established as an acquisition fund, with monies collected from the yearly dues of the Friends of the Art Museum. Beginning in 1996, the Friends of the Art Museum designated that one-third of the fund be used for acquisitions and two-thirds for education programs at the Museum.

THE CHRISTIAN A. JOHNSON
MEMORIAL FUND (1972)

THE REVA B. SEYBOLT '72 ART
ACQUISITION FUND (1972)

THE G. CROSSAN SEYBOLT '77 ART
ACQUISITION FUND (1978)

THE MEMORIAL ART FUND (1980)
Established as a permanent endowment fund to support art acquisitions for Middlebury College's permanent teaching collection.

THE CALVERT H. SEYBOLT '80 ART
ACQUISITION FUND (1986)

THE FREDERICK AND MARTHA
LAPHAM ART ACQUISITION FUND
(1986)
Established as a permanently endowed fund, the income from which is to be used for the acquisition of works of art for Middlebury College.

WALTER CERF ACQUISITION FUND
(1986)
Established as a permanently endowed fund, the income from which is to be used for purchase of works of art for Middlebury College.

THE BARBARA P. AND ROBERT P. '64
YOUNGMAN ACQUISITION FUND FOR
ASIAN ART (1995)
Established as a permanently endowed fund, with one-half the income to be used for acquisitions of Asian works of art for Middlebury College, and one-half for maintenance of the Asian Collection.

THE BARBARA P. AND ROBERT P. '64
YOUNGMAN EXHIBITION FUND (1997)
Established as an endowed fund, the income from which is to be used to support the cost of construction and production of exhibitions of Asian art.

ARTHUR AND HELEN BAER FOUNDA-
TION MUSEUM EDUCATION PROGRAM
SUPPORT FUND (2000)

WILLIAM S. AND ELSIE YOUNGMAN
FUND (2001)

SABRA H. FIELD '57 COLLECTION
ENDOWMENT FUND (2002)

FOSTER FAMILY ART ACQUISITION
FUND (2007)
Established as an endowment fund by Audrey and
James Foster P'06 in honor of the Foster Family.
Supports art acquisitions at the Middlebury Col-
lege Museum of Art with preference for contempo-
rary art, defined as art created within the previous
25 years on a rolling basis.

THE BARBARA P. AND ROBERT P. '64
YOUNGMAN INTERNSHIP FUND (2007)
Established as an endowed fund to provide support for students pursuing internships in the visual
arts in China.

Complete List of Acquisitions Purchased with Funds from the Friends of the Art Museum

* Indicates objects that were included in the exhibition *Friends Bearing Gifts: 40 Years of Acquisitions from the Friends of the Art Museum*

1

Winged Genie Pollinating the Date Palm
Assyrian, Nimrud (Kalhu),
reign of Ashurnasirpal II (883–859 B.C.E.)
Alabaster
94 × 90 inches
Gift of Dr. Wilson A. Farnsworth,
Class of 1848, 0.114
The restoration of this relief was made possible in part by funds raised in 1989 by the Friends of Art at Middlebury College in celebration of their twentieth anniversary. Additional funds were provided by the Getty Grant Program and American Greetings.
See Fig. 44

2*

Lekythos
Greek, late 6th century B.C.E.
Terracotta
H. 9 inches
Purchase with funds provided by the Friends of Art Acquisition Fund, 1969.019
See Fig. 16

3*

Hiram Powers (American, 1805–1873)
Bust of Greek Slave, c. 1850–73
Marble
24½ × 16 × 7½ inches
Gift of the Friends of Art and the Salomon-Hutzler Foundation, 1970.006
See Fig. 18

4*

Mirror
Chinese, Warring States period (475–221 B.C.E.)
Bronze
Dia. 5⁹/₁₆ inches
Purchase with funds provided by the Friends of Art Acquisition Fund, 1971.001

5

Ragini Madhumahari
Indian, Rajasthan, c. 1700
Gouache on paper
8½ × 6 inches
Purchase with funds provided by the Friends of Art Acquisition Fund, 1971.002

6*

Two Scenes from the Life of Buddha
Gandharan (northeastern Pakistan and southern Afghanistan), 2nd–3rd century
Stone
16 × 14 inches
Purchase with funds provided by the Friends of Art Acquisition Fund, 1972.002
See page 40

7

Harvey Breverman (American, born 1934)
Newcomer and the Honors, 1972
Etching on paper
23¼ × 35¾ inches
Purchase with funds provided by the Friends of Art Acquisition Fund, 1973.002

8*

Jan Saenredam (Dutch, 1565–1607)
Jael and Sisera, 16th century
Engraving on paper
11¼ × 7¾ inches
Purchase with funds provided by the Friends of Art Acquisition Fund, 1973.040

9*

Karl Schmidt-Rottluff (German, 1884–1976)
Woman's Head, 1916
Woodcut on paper
11¾ × 8¼ inches
Purchase with funds provided by the Friends
of Art Acquisition Fund, 1973.041

10

Georges Braque (French, 1882–1963)
La Magie Quotidienne, 1959
Etching on paper
12¾ × 20 inches
Purchase with funds provided by the Friends
of Art Acquisition Fund, the Electra Havemeyer
Webb Memorial Fund, and the Christian A.
Johnson Memorial Fund, 1973.042

11

Georges Rouault (French, 1871–1958)
Debout les Morts, 1927
Etching on paper
25½ × 19¾ inches
Purchase with funds provided by the Friends
of Art Acquisition Fund, the Electra Havemeyer
Webb Memorial Fund, and the Christian A.
Johnson Memorial Fund, 1973.043

12*

Raigo Amida and His Host
Japanese, 14th century
Hanging scroll; ink on silk
31 × 13½ inches
Purchase with funds provided by the Friends
of Art Acquisition Fund, 1973.044

13

Yang Ch'Ang-I (Chinese, 19th century)
Landscape
Ink on silk
9½ inches
Purchase with funds provided by the Friends
of Art Acquisition Fund, 1973.045

14

Fish
Chinese, Zhou dynasty (1050–221 B.C.E.)
Jade
3³/16 × 1 inches
Purchase with funds provided by the Friends
of Art Acquisition Fund, 1973.046

15

Pietro Longhi (Italian, 1702–1785)
Commedia dell'Arte Actor with Children Watching,
18th century
Pencil, ink, and wash on paper
10⅞ × 8 inches
Purchase with funds provided by the Friends
of Art Acquisition Fund, 1973.047

16

Paul Delamain (French , 1821–1882)
Study of Open Tents with Seated Figures,
19th century
Pencil on paper
13¼ × 19¾ inches
Purchase with funds provided by the Friends
of Art Acquisition Fund, 1973.048

17*

Haniwa Horse Head
Japanese, 3rd–5th century
Clay
6½ × 12¼ inches
Purchase with funds provided by the Friends
of Art Acquisition Fund, 1974.011

18

Okumura Masanobu (Japanese, 1686–1764)
Aspects of Beauty, 18th century
Woodblock on paper
12¾ × 24 inches
Purchase with funds provided by the Friends
of Art Acquisition Fund, 1974.019

19*

Hannes Beckmann (American, 1909–1977)
Twice, 1971
Oil on canvas
30 × 25 inches
Purchase with funds provided by the Friends of
Art Acquisition Fund and a matching grant from
the National Endowment for the Arts, 1976.002

20*

Philip Pearlstein (American, born 1924)
Girl on Iron Bench, 1974
Lithograph on paper
24¾ × 34¼ inches
Purchase with funds provided by the Friends of
Art Acquisition Fund and a matching grant from
the National Endowment for the Arts, 1976.142

21

21*

Willem de Kooning (American, born the Netherlands, 1904–1997)
High School Desk, 1970
Lithograph on paper
40 × 28 inches
Purchase with funds provided by the Friends of Art Acquisition Fund and a matching grant from the National Endowment for the Arts, 1976.143
(Photo: Tad Merrick)

22

Frank Stella (American, born 1936)
Sandornville, 1974
Lithograph on paper
17¼ × 22¼ inches
Purchase with funds provided by the Friends of Art Acquisition Fund and a matching grant from the National Endowment for the Arts, 1976.144

23*

Ellsworth Kelly (American, born 1923)
Blue/Green/Black/Red, 1971
Lithograph on paper
30 × 27½ inches
Purchase with funds provided by the Friends of Art Acquisition Fund and a matching grant from the National Endowment for the Arts, 1976.145
(Photo: Tad Merrick)

24

Robert Mangold (American, born 1937)
Distorted Circle within a Polygon, 1973
Serigraph on paper
14½ × 14½ inches
Purchase with funds provided by the Friends of Art Acquisition Fund and a matching grant from the National Endowment for the Arts, 1976.146

25

Alex Katz (American, born 1927)
Day Lily, 1969
Lithograph on paper
21 × 28 inches
Purchase with funds provided by the Friends of Art Acquisition Fund and a matching grant from the National Endowment for the Arts, 1976.147

23

26
Hugh Kepets (American, born 1946)
Eighth Avenue, 1976
Serigraph on paper
45 × 35 inches
Purchase with funds provided by the Friends of
Art Acquisition Fund and a matching grant from
the National Endowment for the Arts, 1976.148

27
Roy Lichtenstein (American, 1923–1997)
Crak!, 1964
Serigraph on paper
18½ × 27 inches
Purchase with funds provided by the Friends of
Art Acquisition Fund and a matching grant from
the National Endowment for the Arts, 1976.149

28
Richard Anuszkiewicz (American, born 1930)
Spectral Cadmium, 1968
Serigraph on paper
26¾ × 26¾ inches
Purchase with funds provided by the Friends of
Art Acquisition Fund and a matching grant from
the National Endowment for the Arts, 1976.150

29*
Andy Warhol (American, 1928–1987)
Soup Can (Vegetable Made with Beef Stock), 1968
Serigraph on paper
34⅞ × 22⅞ inches
Purchase with funds provided by the Friends of
Art Acquisition Fund and a matching grant from
the National Endowment for the Arts, 1976.151
(Photo: Tad Merrick)

30
Robert Rauschenberg (American, born 1925)
Sky Hook, 1969
Lithograph on paper
48 × 34 inches
Purchase with funds provided by the Friends of
Art Acquisition Fund and a matching grant from
the National Endowment for the Arts, 1976.152

31*
Jasper Johns (American, born 1930)
Flags II, 1973
Serigraph on paper
7⅜ × 36⅜ inches
Purchase with funds provided by the Friends of
Art Acquisition Fund and a matching grant from
the National Endowment for the Arts, 1976.154

32
Jim Dine (American, born 1935)
Bathrobe, 1975
Woodblock and lithograph on paper
35½ × 24 inches
Purchase with funds provided by the Friends of
Art Acquisition Fund and a matching grant from
the National Endowment for the Arts, 1976.159

33
George Rickey (American, 1907–2002)
Two Open Rectangles, Excentric, Variation VI, 1976
Stainless steel
12 × 3 feet
Purchase with funds provided by the Friends of
Art Acquisition Fund and a matching grant from
the National Endowment for the Arts, 1977.002

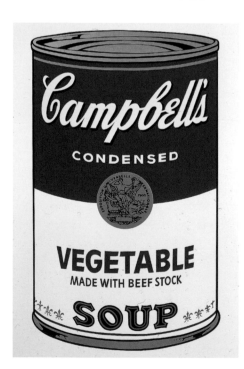

29

34
Celadon Bowl
Chinese, Song dynasty (960–1279)
Porcelain
Dia. 8⅛ inches
Purchase with funds provided by the Friends
of Art Acquisition Fund, 1978.008

35*
Chuck Close (American, born 1940)
Self Portrait, 1977
Etching and aquatint on paper
44½ × 35½ inches
Purchase with funds provided by the Friends of
Art Acquisition Fund and a matching grant from
the National Endowment for the Arts, 1978.018
(Photo: Tad Merrick)

36*
François Rude (French, 1784–1855)
Bust of a Man (Head of a Gaul), after 1883
Bronze
6¼ × 8¾ × 11 inches
Purchase with funds provided by the Friends
of Art Acquisition Fund, 1979.020

37*
Jean-Alexandre-Joseph Falguière (French,
1831–1900)
Bust of Diana, 1880s
Bronze
17¾ × 18½ × 15 inches
Purchase with funds provided by the Friends
of Art Acquisition Fund, 1979.021
See Fig. 19

38*
Jean-Baptiste Greuze (French, 1725–1805)
Study of an Old Man (The Village Betrothal), c. 1763
Red chalk on paper
18 × 14½ inches
Gift of the Friends of Art, 1980.004

39*
Govaert Flinck (Dutch, 1615–1660)
Portrait of a Man, 17th century
Oil on panel
21⅝ × 16¼ inches
Gift of the Friends of Art, 1981.006
(Photo: Arthur Evans)

39

40
William Mason Brown (American, 1828–1898)
In the Alleghenies, c. 1870
Oil on canvas
10¼ × 14¼ inches
Gift of the Friends of Art, 1982.012

41*
Pieter Cornelis Dommershuijzen
(Dutch, 1834–1908)
Coastal Shipping, 1876
Oil on canvas
19¼ × 31½ inches
Gift of the Friends of Art, 1983.010

42*
John Byam Liston Shaw (British, 1872–1919)
The Lady of Shallot, 1898
Oil on panel
13¼ × 10³/16 inches
Gift of the Friends of Art, 1984.026
(Photo: Tad Merrick)

43

42

43*
Enkolpion
Eastern Mediterranean, perhaps Syria, Middle
Byzantine, 9th–10th century
Bronze
5⅞ × 3 inches
Gift of the Friends of Art, 1985.009
(Photo: Ken Burris)

44*
Richard Ryan (American, born 1950)
Still Life with Four Figures, 1984
Oil on canvas
76 × 64½ inches
Gift of the Friends of Art, 1986.078
(Photo: Tad Merrick)

45

John Kingsbury (American, active 1860s)
The Army Relief Group, 1864
Albumen print
5½ × 7½ inches
Gift of the Friends of Art, 1987.038

46

Charles Fredericks (American, 1823–1894)
Peter Sturgis, 1857
Wax salt print
8 × 6¼ inches
Gift of the Friends of Art, 1987.039

47

Alexander Gardner (American, 1821–1882)
Cabin Scene with Artist, 1864
Albumen print
6¼ × 9 inches
Gift of the Friends of Art, 1987.040

48

William Bell (American, 1839–1915)
Wounded Soldier, 1865
Albumen print
7½ × 6½ inches
Gift of the Friends of Art, 1987.041

44

49

49*

Alexander Gardner (American, 1821–1882)
The Surgeons, 1864
Albumen print
7 × 9 inches
Gift of the Friends of Art, 1987.042
(Photo: Tad Merrick)

50

Mathew Brady (American, 1823–1896)
The Reverend, 1854
Salt print
9½ × 7½ inches
Gift of the Friends of Art, 1987.043

51

Mathew Brady (American, 1823–1896)
A Military Officer, 1859
Salt print
9 × 5 15/16 inches
Gift of the Friends of Art, 1987.044

52

Timothy H. O'Sullivan (American, 1840–1882)
The Old Trapper, 1869
Albumen print
8⅝ × 11¼ inches
Gift of the Friends of Art, 1987.045

56

53
Andrew Joseph Russell (American, 1830–1902)
The Rock Great Eastern, 1869
Albumen print
8½ × 11 inches
Gift of the Friends of Art, 1987.046

54
Alexander Gardner (American, 1821–1882)
Camp Oneida Company, 1864
Albumen print
7 × 9⅜ inches
Gift of the Friends of Art, 1987.047

55
John K. Hillers (American, 1843–1925)
Big Mouth, 1875
Albumen print
9¼ × 7 inches
Gift of the Friends of Art, 1987.048

56*
Mathew Brady (American, 1823–1896)
The Sanitary Commission, 1864
Salt print mixed with gum
9⅞ × 15⅞ inches
Gift of the Friends of Art, 1987.049
(Photo: Tad Merrick)

57*
Max Weber (American, 1881–1961)
Dining, 1913
Pastel on paper
24½ × 18¾ inches
Purchase with funds provided by the Friends of
Art Acquisition Fund and the Christian A. Johnson
Memorial Fund, 1988.131
(Photo: Tad Merrick)

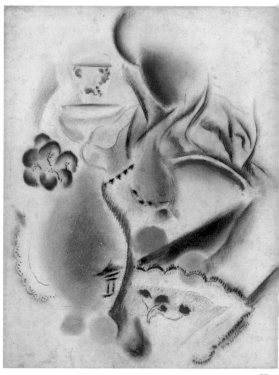

57

58

59

58*
Giuseppe De Nittis (Italian, 1846–1884)
Study for Alle Corse, c. 1874
Oil on panel
5 × 9¼ inches
Purchase with funds provided by the Friends of
Art Acquisition Fund and the Christian A. Johnson
Memorial Fund, 1989.007
(Photo: Tad Merrick)

59*
William Davis (British, 1812–1873)
Shotwick Church, Cheshire, 1855
Oil on panel
13 × 20 inches
Purchase with funds provided by the Friends of
Art Acquisition Fund and the Christian A. Johnson
Memorial Fund, 1990.040
(Photo: Ken Burris)

60

60*
Attic Black-Figure Amphora
Greek, Attic, c. 530–520 B.C.E.
Circle of The Antimenes Painter
Terracotta
H. 15⅝, dia. 10 inches
Purchase with funds provided by the Friends of
Art Acquisition Fund, the Christian A. Johnson
Memorial Fund, the Walter Cerf Art Fund, and the
Memorial Art Fund, 1991.002
(Photo: Ken Burris)

61*
*Child's Sarcophagus with Relief Depicting Scenes from
the Hippolytus Myth*
Roman, 210–220 C.E.
Marble
12 × 45 × 16 inches
Purchase with funds provided by the Friends of
Art Acquisition Fund, the Overbrook Foundation,
and the Memorial Art Fund, 1993.001

63

62
Philibert Louis Debucourt (French, 1755–1832)
Les Deux Baisers (*The Two Kisses*), 1786
Etching with engraving and tool work on paper
14 × 16¾ inches
Purchase with funds provided by the Friends of
Art Acquisition Fund, 1993.015

63*
Jean Mathieu (French, 1749–1815)
After Jean-Honore Fragonard (French, 1734–1806)
Le Serment d'Amour (*The Oath of Love*), 1786
Etching with engraving on paper
23⅛ × 17⁹/₁₆ inches
Purchase with funds provided by the Friends
of Art Acquisition Fund and the Frederick and
Martha Lapham Art Acquisition Fund, 1993.016
(Photo: Tad Merrick)

67

64[*]

William Zorach (American, born Lithuania,
1889–1966)
Kiddie Kar, c. 1923
Rosewood
18¼ × 13⅞ × 8 inches
Purchase with funds provided by the Friends of
Art Acquisition Fund and the Christian A. Johnson
Memorial Fund, 1994.007
See page 62

65

Timothy H. O'Sullivan (American, 1840–1882)
Print by Alexander Gardner (American, 1821–1882)
A Harvest of Death, at the Battle of Gettysburg., July
1863
Albumen print
6¾ × 8⅞ inches
Purchase with funds provided by the Friends
of Art Acquisition Fund, 1995.018

66

Eadweard Muybridge (British, 1830–1904)
Loya, Valley of Yosemite, c. 1872
Albumen print
17 × 21⅝ inches
Purchase with funds provided by the Friends
of Art Acquisition Fund, 1998.030

67[*]

The Betrayal of Christ
British, c. 1500
Alabaster with traces of paint
15 × 11⅜ × 2⅞ inches
Purchase with funds provided by the Friends
of Art Acquisition Fund, 2000.027

68

68*
*Diptych with Scenes of the Nativity and the
Crucifixion*
French, mid-14th century
Ivory with traces of paint
3¹/₁₆ × 4⅞ inches
Purchase with funds provided by the Friends of
Art Acquisition Fund; the Frederick and Martha
Lapham Art Acquisition Fund; and Margery
Lehmann, Class of 1948, and Allen Stillman,
2002.013
(Photo: Ken Burris)

69
Aryballos
Corinthian, Early Archaic Period (c. 575 B.C.E.)
Terracotta
H. 4½ inches
Purchase with funds provided by the Walter Cerf
Art Acquisition Fund, the Frederick and Martha
Lapham Art Acquisition Fund, and the Friends of
Art Acquisition Fund, 2002.025

70*
Caparisoned Horse
Chinese, Eastern Wei dynasty (534–550 C.E.)
Earthenware with traces of pigments
12¾ × 12½ × 7¾ inches
Purchase with funds provided by the Friends
of Art Acquisition Fund, 2004.015
See page 2

71*
Harry Bertoia (American, 1915–1978)
Sounding Sculpture, c. 1970–78
Beryllium copper and brass
45½ × 10 × 10 inches
Purchase with funds provided by the Friends of
Art Acquisition Fund, the Christian A. Johnson
Memorial Fund, and gift (by exchange) of
Carmen Walker '11, Wilbur F. Weeks '47, Prudence
Montgomery, and Mr. and Mrs. Lawrence McCoy,
2005.049

72*
Figure of Venus
Roman, Hadrianic Period, c. 118–136 C.E.
Bronze with traces of gilding
H. 5½ inches
Purchase with funds provided by the Friends
of Art Acquisition Fund, 2005.053
See page 6

76

73
Fragment of a Lotus Sutra
Chinese, Dunhuang, 7th century
Hand scroll; ink on paper
H. 10⅝ inches
Joint purchase of the Middlebury College Museum
of Art and Middlebury College Special Collections
with funds provided by the Friends of Art
Acquisition Fund and the Friends of the Library,
2006.020

74*
Anne Lilly (American, born 1966)
Leda, 2005
Stainless steel
24 × 14 × 14 inches (24 × 28 × 28 inches in motion)
Purchase with funds provided by the Friends of
Art Acquisition Fund, 2007.033

75*
Canopic Jar of Pa-Iynen
Egyptian, possibly from Thebes, New Kingdom,
Dynasty XVIII, c. 1550–1295 B.C.E.
Ceramic
H. 13⅜ inches
Purchase with funds provided by the Friends
of Art Acquisition Fund, 2008.035

76*
Head of the Wounded Amazon
of Polykleitos of Argos
Greek, Late Classical/Early Hellenistic,
late 4th to early 3rd century B.C.E.
Copy of a High Classical original sculpture,
c. 440–430 B.C.E.
Greek marble
H. 3⅜ × 3³/₁₆ × 3½ inches
Purchase with funds provided by the Friends
of Art Acquisition Fund, 2009.001
(Photo: Tad Merrick)

William Zorach, 1889–1966, *Kiddie Kar*, c. 1923, rosewood, 18¼ × 13⅞ × 8 inches. Purchase with funds provided by the Friends of Art Acquisition Fund and the Christian A. Johnson Memorial Fund, 1994.007. (Photo: Erik Borg)

Bibliography

Annual Reports and **Newsletters** published by Middlebury College:

The Johnson Gallery News. 1969.

Annual Report of the Johnson Gallery, 1970; 1971; 1972–1973; 1974; 1975; 1976; 1977; 1978; 1979; 1980; 1981.

The Christian A. Johnson Memorial Gallery of Middlebury College Annual Report. 1982; 1983; 1984; 1985; 1986; 1987; 1988; 1989; 1990; 1991.

Arts at Middlebury College. Vols. 1–16 (October/November 1991–Winter 2007). Newsletter published by Middlebury College.

Arts at Middlebury. Vols. 16–19 (Fall/Winter 2007–Spring 2010). Newsletter published by Middlebury College.

Friends of Art Newsletter. Winter 1984–1986. One-page letter [mimeographed].

Friends of Art Christian A. Johnson Memorial Gallery. Newsletter. Vols. 1–7 (Summer 1986–Winter/Spring 1992). Newsletter published by Middlebury College.

Friends of the Art Museum. Newsletter. Vols. 7 13 (Fall 1992/Winter 1993–Winter/Spring 1999). Newsletter published by Middlebury College. Fall 1997 incorporates 1996 *Annual Report.* Fall 1998/Winter 1999 incorporates 1997 *Annual Report.*

Middlebury College Museum of Art Annual Reports. Published by Middlebury College. 1992; 1993; 1994; 1998–99; 2000–2001; 2002–2003; 2003–2004.

Interviews

David Bumbeck, Middlebury, Vermont. April 13, 2010.

Betty Fishman, West Palm Beach, Florida. March 15, 2010 [telephone]

John Hunisak, Middlebury, Vermont. May 5, 2010

Martha Lapham, Middlebury, Vermont. May 14, 2010

Helen Reiff, Middlebury, Vermont. March 25, 2010

A. Richard Turner, Cape May, New Jersey. March 8, 2010 [telephone]

Resources from Special Collections

College Archives, Special Collections Middlebury College, Middlebury, Vermont.

A3 2.1 V-P/Dir. of Dev., Corresp. Friends of Art 1967–70.
A3 2.1 V-P/Dir. of Dev., Corresp. Friends of Art 1974–78.
A3 2.1 V-P/Dir. of Dev., Corresp. Fine Arts Dept., 1970–74.
A3 2.2 Development Office Records, Johnson Gallery, 1970–89.
A3 2.2 Development Office Records, Friends of Art, 1982–85.
A3 2.2 Development Office Records, Johnson Memorial Scholarship Fund, 1964–69.
A12 PF Christian A. Johnson Memorial Building 1968 Dedication.
A12 1 Middlebury College Buildings A-J, Johnson Memorial Building.
Borg Photographic Collection.

Stameshkin, David M. *The Strength of the Hills: Middlebury College, 1915–1990.* Hanover, New Hampshire, 1996.

This exhibition catalogue celebrates the
fortieth anniversary of the Friends of the Art Museum.
Printed by Capital Offset, Concord, New Hampshire.
Composed in Arno and Magma types.
Designed by Christopher Kuntze.